Member  king Group of ... Guidelines for Schoo. .ieals

Acknowledgements

The Working Group would like to thank Ms Ashley Adamson, Mr Tim Butler, Mr Geoffrey Cannon, Ms Gill Cawdron, Professor John Garrow, Mr Gerard McAlea, Ms Hilary Whent and Dr Jennifer Woolfe for their contributions to this report.

The Caroline Walker Trust would like to thank the Health Education Authority, Sir Emmanuel Kaye, and Safeway plc, for providing the financial support, in the form of unconditional grants, which has made this report possible.

Terms of reference

The Expert Working Group on Nutritional Guidelines for School Meals was established in 1992 by The Caroline Walker Trust, with the following terms of reference:

- To review the past and current contribution of school meals to the diets of British school children

- To review briefly the contribution of school meals to the health of British school children

- To consider the potential contribution of school meals to the diets of school children

- To review the implementation and effectiveness of nutritional standards

- To develop new guidelines consistent with recent government dietary recommendations (Dietary Reference Values)

- To make broad recommendations on the implementation of the new guidelines.

Contents

List of Tables and Figures

TABLES

FIGURES

Foreword

Every nation has a duty to maintain and protect the health of its children – its next generation of citizens. Children need a nourishing diet to maintain and protect their health now, and throughout their lives. But it is well known that the average diet eaten in industrialised societies such as the UK is an important contributor to many disorders and diseases, some of which can prove fatal. This report, which sets nutritional guidelines for school meals in the UK, is therefore of vital and urgent importance.

A healthy diet includes plenty of vegetables and fruit, cereals, bread (preferably wholegrain) and other starchy foods. Foods of animal origin such as meat and dairy products are fine as long as they are relatively low in fat. But the typical British diet contains too much fat (especially hard, saturated fat), and too much sugar and salt. Such a diet is an important reason why British people suffer high rates not only of diseases that usually show in middle and old age, such as heart disease and certain forms of cancers, but also of disorders and diseases that can begin in childhood or early adult life, such as tooth decay, constipation and obesity.

Reliable surveys consistently show that the diets of British school children are high in fat, sugar and salt, and often worryingly low in some vitamins and minerals necessary for healthy growth and development. Scientists agree that prevention of diseases of middle and old age such as heart attacks, stroke, diabetes, osteoporosis and cancers, is best begun as early in life as possible. The best protection against such diseases is a healthy lifestyle and diet, right from the start of life.

The purpose of this report is to provide a sound nutritional basis for modern school catering. These nutritional guidelines for the provision of school meals will, if used, enable children to eat a healthy diet in school. If the recommendations of this report are put into practice, they will help to protect the nation's health.

The British government is now formally and firmly committed to a policy designed to encourage a healthy national diet. This has given a firm foundation for the work of The Caroline Walker Trust Expert Working Group, in setting these nutritional guidelines for school meals adapted from officially agreed recommendations.

The purpose of The Caroline Walker Trust is to improve public health by means of good food. Established in 1988, it is named after the pioneering nutritionist Caroline Walker, who throughout her life campaigned for a better British diet. The Trust is a founder member of the School Meals Campaign.

Publication of this report has been made possible by many individual donations and notably by unconditional grants from the Health Education Authority, Sir Emmanuel Kaye, and Safeway plc. The Trust is a registered charity whose work is wholly dependent on gifts and donations. Please address any enquiries to: The Caroline Walker Trust, 6 Aldridge Road Villas, London W11 1BP.

Maggie Sanderson
Chair
The Caroline Walker Trust

Geoffrey Cannon
Secretary
The Caroline Walker Trust

Summary

The overall aim of these nutritional guidelines for school meals is to contribute to a diet which contains more bread, cereals and other starchy foods, more fruit and vegetables, and less fat, sugar and salty foods, and which is richer in minerals and vitamins.

The guidelines provide figures for the recommended nutrient content of an average school meal provided for children over a one-week period. In practical terms this is the total amount of food provided, divided by the number of children eating it, averaged over a week.

Table 1	SUMMARY OF NUTRITIONAL GUIDELINES FOR SCHOOL MEALS
ENERGY	30% of the Estimated Average Requirement (EAR)
FAT	Not more than 35% of food energy
SATURATED FATTY ACIDS	Not more than 11% of food energy
CARBOHYDRATE	Not less than 50% of food energy
NON-MILK EXTRINSIC SUGARS	Not more than 11% of food energy
NSP ('fibre')	Not less than 30% of the Calculated Reference Value
PROTEIN	Not less than 30% of the Reference Nutrient Intake (RNI)
IRON	Not less than 40% of the Reference Nutrient Intake (RNI)
CALCIUM	Not less than 35% of the Reference Nutrient Intake (RNI)
VITAMIN A (retinol equivalents)	Not less than 30% of the Reference Nutrient Intake (RNI)
FOLATE	Not less than 40% of the Reference Nutrient Intake (RNI)
VITAMIN C	Not less than 35% of the Reference Nutrient Intake (RNI)
Sodium should be reduced in catering practice.	

Further details are provided in Chapter 6. The full tables are given in Appendix 4 (Tables 12-20). A list of rich sources of nutrients is given in Appendix 3.

CHAPTER I

Introduction

"From the point of view of the State, the adoption of a standard of diet lower than the optimum is uneconomic. It leads to a great amount of preventable disease and ill-health which lay a heavy financial burden on the State ..."
From *Food, health and income*, by Boyd Orr, 1937

Background

Concern for the health and welfare of children, especially the poor, first led to the provision of school dinners by charities in the 19th century. Ever since that time, school meals have been considered important for social, nutritional and educational reasons.

The school meals service was introduced in 1906, following the discovery of severe malnutrition among recruits for the Boer War, and an awareness that many children were attending school underfed and thus unable to benefit from formal education. By the second World War, the service had developed into large-scale provision of a standardised meal at a standard charge, and these are the main lines on which it has operated for much of the time since. Throughout the 20th century, the school meals service has responded to the changing social, economic and political climate.

The Education Act in 1980 marked a major policy shift in the provision of lunches for children, and much of the central control was relinquished. The Act removed the obligation of local education authorities (LEAs) to provide school meals for all children, and to provide meals at a particular price and of a particular quality. LEAs were thus left to determine the cost and nutritional standard of school meals. The only statutory requirement was to provide free meals for children who were entitled to them.

Since 1980, however, pressure has built up for a return to nutritional standards for school meals. Numerous scientific reports have outlined the case for a healthy diet that is low in fat, sugar and salt, and high in fibre, with plenty of starchy foods and fruit and vegetables, and have emphasised the need for this to begin in childhood. Most recently, the government's strategy for health, *The health of the nation*, sets targets for improving the nation's diet, and for reducing diet-related ill health, including the major causes of death – coronary heart disease, stroke and some cancers. The nutritional concerns may have changed since the turn of the century, but the case for the contribution of school meals to a healthy diet remains.

The 1980 Education Act was a response to financial circumstances, innovations in provision, and concerns about wasted food. However, school meal provision has changed substantially since that time, with the widespread use of cash cafeterias in secondary schools and the introduction of compulsory competitive tendering. But experience shows that if nutritional quality is built into the tendering process – in specifications, menu planning and monitoring – it is possible to provide healthy meals at school which are also financially viable.

About this report

This report aims to help improve the overall nutritional quality of school meals, by providing quantified nutritional guidelines. The recommendations are based on evidence on the overall nutritional content of children's diets and the health implications of these diets, both in childhood and later life, and the expert judgement of the Working Group, convened by The Caroline Walker Trust, on the contribution that school meals should make.

The report represents a first step in improving the nutritional content of school meals. It is intended for policy makers in government, education, health and catering, and others working to improve school meals provision.

These nutritional guidelines for school meals are informed by the government's Dietary Reference Values (DRVs), published in 1991, which set out quantified nutritional guidelines for the UK population, including children. These updated the earlier Recommended Daily Amounts (RDAs).

The report provides recommended quantified guidelines for the nutritional content of an *average* school meal, based on menus covering a one-week period. Appropriate and practical recommendations are made for school meals for children from different age and sex groups. They are not intended as a return to the pre-1980 nutritional standards, which applied to the content of the meal eaten by each child: it is impractical to set such guidelines for each plate of food provided, particularly within the current system. Patterns of eating have changed, and children now have far more choice. Furthermore, not all nutrients need to be eaten every day. These guidelines should thus be applied to the overall food provided in school meals, and the average meal provided in a week. In practical terms this is the total amount of food, divided by the number of children eating it, averaged over a week.

The guidelines are in line with current catering practices and nutritional recommendations, and provide an achievable goal in school meal provision. They will be useful for those involved in establishing and monitoring specifications for school meals, in menu planning, and in provision.

Figure 1   **USING THE NUTRITIONAL GUIDELINES**

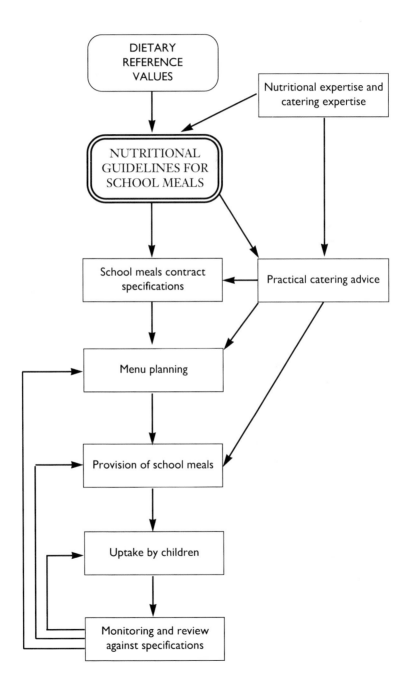

The next step

The next step will be the implementation of the nutritional guidelines for school meals, which need to be translated into qualitative guidelines and practical advice for caterers. While broad recommendations for implementation are given in Chapter 7, this report does not address practical implementation in detail. Improvements in school meals should also be set within the context of a health promoting school (see Chapter 3).

There are many different ways in which school caterers could achieve the guidelines, and provide healthy meals which children choose. Compulsory competitive tendering represents an opportunity for improving quality. While the challenges may be different in primary and secondary schools, in the set canteen meal and the cash cafeteria meal, encouraging uptake of nutritious school meals is an important challenge for all.

The Caroline Walker Trust is a founder member of the School Meals Campaign, which recommends the reintroduction of nationally agreed nutritional standards for the provision of all school meals. This report aims to make that possible.

CHAPTER 2

A history of school meal provision

SUMMARY

Concern about under-nutrition among children at the beginning of this century led to the introduction in 1906 of the school meal service, which aimed to benefit undernourished and needy children. The service grew in scope throughout the first half of the century and, by the end of the second World War, had become a general service for all children, with government grants to LEAs covering 95% of the cost of providing the meals. The first nutritional standards for school meals were set in 1941.

The Education Act (1944) made it the duty of all local education authorities (LEAs) to provide school meals for those who wanted them and, for the next 20 years, LEAs became agents of central government in providing a standard school meal at a set price. From 1947 the full net cost of school meals was met by the government. Free milk, supplied to needy school children since 1934, became available to all school children in 1946.

In 1950, the principle of a standard charge for the school meal was introduced, with remission arrangements for those unable to pay. This principle was not abandoned until 1980. In 1967, financial responsibility for the school meals service passed to the LEAs, resulting in loss of central control and giving LEAs greater discretion over the meals provided and the pricing policy. Since 1967, there have been successive increases in the charge for the school meal, and restrictions in the supply of free school milk.

The 1980 Education Act is an important milestone in the history of school meals: it removed the obligation on LEAs to provide school meals, except for children entitled to free school meals; and it removed the obligation for meals to be sold at a fixed price, and for them to meet any nutritional standards. The 1986 Social Security Act limited the number of children entitled to free school meals, and in 1988 the Local Government Act introduced compulsory competitive tendering, obliging LEAs to put school meals services out to tender.

The origins of the school meal service can be traced back to the work of charities in the mid-19th century. The Destitute Children's Dinner Society was founded in 1864 and by the end of the decade had established 58 dining rooms in London. Other charities followed suit.

Compulsory education began in Britain in 1880, and brought to light the problem of underfed children. School meals were provided at that time by voluntary workers, including teachers, who helped ensure that the children most in need were fed, especially during winter and periods of unemployment. At the turn of the century, many schools were already providing some food for the many pupils who found it impossible to go home at midday. Provision tended to be regarded as the responsibility of the school rather than the local education authority (LEA).

Public concern, however, was not widely stirred until 1904, with the disclosure of severe malnutrition in recruits for the Boer War in South Africa, and the report of the Royal Commission on Physical Deterioration. This led eventually to the Education (Provision of Meals) Act in 1906, which aimed to supply food to children who would otherwise have had to go without, and whose education would have suffered as a result.

The principles on which the school meals service has operated for much of the last 50 years were laid down during the second World War, and the period of food shortage that followed it. This involved the provision, on a large scale, of a broadly standardised meal, at a uniform charge, with remission arrangements for cases of hardship. Changes in the economic climate after the second World War, and the wider provision of social welfare benefits, have led to successive increases in the charge for the school meal, and restrictions in the supply of free school meals.

As a wider range of foods became available, the importance of the school meal for most children's nutrition decreased. However, the nutritional status and needs of children have also changed: the emphasis of concern has shifted from under-nutrition to over-consumption of calorie-dense foods, high in fats and sugars, leading to overweight, tooth decay and other chronic disorders such as cardiovascular diseases and some cancers.

This chapter outlines a chronological history of policy and provision of food in schools, including meals and milk, during the 20th century.

1904

The report of an Inter-Departmental Committee on Physical Deterioration was published, which commented on the causes of the poor physique of volunteers for the South African (Boer) war, and reached the conclusion that "on a general survey of the evidence ... the Committee think that a large number of children habitually attend school ill-fed."

1905

The publication of the report of the Inter-Departmental Committee on

Medical Inspection and Feeding of Children attending Public Elementary Schools shed light on the prevalence of under-feeding.

1906

These reports, which focused public concern on under-nutrition among children, led to the introduction of the Education (Provision of Meals) Act (1906) in England and Wales. The primary aim of this Act was educational: to ensure that insufficient food did not prevent children from benefitting from education.

The Act gave all local education authorities (LEAs) for elementary education the power to provide meals free or at a reduced price for children who needed them, and to others at a charge no less than the cost of the food. The Act permitted, but did not compel, LEAs to provide meals.

In Scotland, the Education (Provision of Meals) Act, introduced in 1908, made similar provisions.

For about the next 30 years, the provision of meals in elementary schools was aimed almost exclusively at the needy child. If meals were also provided for children who paid, they were often better, and provided in a separate place.

1914-18

At the onset of the first World War in 1914, some 160,000 children were taking school meals. However, in the first year of the war, the expenditure limit for school meals was removed and a grant from the Exchequer of 50% of expenditure was introduced. The number of children taking school meals jumped to half a million. In Scotland, the Education (Scotland) (Provision of Meals) Act of 1914 attempted to extend the service by enabling school boards to provide meals on non-school days. During the later war years, and immediately post-war, the number of children taking school meals fell to 50,000.

1921-23

In the years of the post-war depression, the number of children taking school meals rose again to 600,000. However, in an effort to economise, the government reduced the total expenditure of LEAs on school meals. The total number of children taking meals fell to 150,000 in 1922-23.

1925-36

In the depression years between 1925 and 1936, anxieties about malnutrition led to renewed administrative encouragement of school meals of all types: lunches, breakfasts, dinners and snacks.

However, a further qualifying criterion for free or reduced cost school meals was introduced in 1934: the child had to be not only poor, but also suffering from some degree of malnutrition. Surveys to detect malnutrition were introduced, and these were used to persuade authorities to increase the service, to help ensure that no child, particularly in low-income groups, was too malnourished to take advantage of formal education.

In 1934 a Milk in Schools Scheme was started by the Milk Marketing Board, in conjunction with the Board of Education. The scheme provided free milk for needy school children and enabled other school children to buy it for a halfpenny for one-third of a pint. This scheme encountered problems in the war years due to shortages of milk, and difficulties in supplying it in a form convenient for schools, and take-up rates fell.

1939

At the start of the second World War, attention was directed mainly to the provision of free meals for undernourished and needy children. However, school meals provision underwent a transformation in terms of policy and scope during the war years, and became a general service of lunchtime meals intended to benefit all children. National policy dictated that a main midday meal would be provided in schools for all children whose parents wanted them to have it, on payment of a charge almost equivalent to the cost of the food, or free of charge in cases of hardship.

There were four reasons for this policy shift:

- Domestic rations took no account of children's special needs.
- Bombing and movement of the population led to the widespread development of civic catering facilities.
- Wartime employment of women made school meals a necessity for many families.
- A new policy of a family allowance included free school meals and milk as benefits.

1940

The Board of Education encouraged authorities to increase the school meals service: the government grant to LEAs was increased to 70%, covering expenditure on meals and allocation of rationed foods. Over the next year, the number of children taking school meals increased by 50%, and the term 'school feeding centre' was replaced by 'school canteen'.

1941

The Board of Education, with the support of the Minister of Food, introduced a general campaign to expand the school meals service to one million meals a day, in England, Wales and Scotland, within a year. To encourage this, the government grant to LEAs was raised to a maximum of 95%; central ordering and purchasing arrangements were introduced; and the school meals service was given priority in the supply of rationed or other foodstuffs, premises and equipment. Financial hardship became the sole criterion for free school meals:

additional evidence of malnutrition was no longer needed.

Also in 1941, the first nutritional standards for school meals were laid down, covering energy, protein and fat. Government Circular 1571 advised LEAs that, in general, a school dinner should be planned to provide a child with:

- 1,000 kilocalories
- 20-25 grams of 'first class' protein
- 30 grams of fat (in all forms).

The circular pointed out that only 'first class' protein and fat were specifically mentioned because the amount of these available during war time was restricted, and most of the daily requirement of these two nutrients should be provided by the school meal. It also pointed out that allowance should be made for probable deficiency of other factors in the home diet.

The milk supply scheme was introduced by the Ministry of Food, which gave priority to school milk, and the Board of Education raised to 100% the grant for the cost of handling school milk, and providing it free to needy children. With widespread publicity, take-up of school milk rose to 75%.

1942

The government campaign reached its target of providing one million school meals a day, and the service continued to expand. The Education (Scotland) Act gave education authorities a new power to pay for and provide food for all school children and to recover the cost in whole or part from parents who could afford it.

1943

The government called for a renewed campaign of expansion of the school meals service, and raised the target for provision to more than three million dinners a day, or 75% of all school children. The main policy mechanism to achieve this was the transfer to central government of the whole cost of establishing and equipping school canteens, and this continued until 1949.

1944

The Education Act (1944) marks an important step forward in the history of school meals. Section 49 of the Act imposed a new, statutory duty on LEAs to provide milk, meals and other refreshment to school children. From 1 April 1945, LEAs were required to provide school meals for all pupils in maintained primary and secondary schools who wanted them. Thus, the Act converted the power of the 1906 Act to a duty covering all pupils of maintained schools, making school meals available to all who wanted them.

The charges made for school meals required ministerial approval, but could not exceed the cost of the food. LEAs were also given the power to provide other meals and to continue the service on weekends and holidays. The school dinners had to be suitable as the main meal of the day, and follow the nutritional specifications set down in 1941.

Thus, for the next 20 years, LEAs were to become agents of central government in providing a standard school meal at a set price, with the net cost provided almost entirely by a grant from the Exchequer.

1945

By 1945 it was clear that the expansion of the school meals service could not continue along improvised lines, and that proper dining room facilities were essential. LEAs were encouraged to plan on a more permanent basis for a service that was now obligatory. A Ministry of Education circular described the school meal as having "a vital place in national policy for the nutrition and well-being of children".

In Scotland, separate legislation, the Education (Scotland) Act (1945), specified that midday meals were to be of good quality, adequate as the main meal of the day for the pupil, well prepared and cooked, attractively served and in good condition.

1946-47

Free milk became available to all school children in 1946, with the introduction of the 'Beveridge' family support arrangements. Each pupil was entitled to one-third of a pint of milk a day, and by October 1946, 92.6% of all school children were taking this. In 1954, LEAs assumed responsibility for this milk.

From 1947, the full net cost of school meals was met by the government, under a new grant system. One year later, a similar grant was introduced in Scotland, to cover all expenditure incurred by local authorities on school meals.

1949

The 75% target for school meals provision set in 1943 was not reached during the war years. By 1949, the numbers of children taking school meals reached about 2.75 million, representing some 52% of the total school population, and the service now covered 27,000 of 29,000 schools or departments. By this time, social and economic improvements had reduced the pressure for free school meals.

1950

In 1950, the principle of a standard charge for the school meal was introduced, with remission arrangements for those unable to pay. This was not abandoned until 1980.

1955

The nutritional standards for school meals were updated in 1955. Government Circular 290 recommended that the school meal should provide:

- 650-1,000 kilocalories, depending on the age and sex of the child
- 20 grams of protein of animal origin, on average
- 25-30 grams of fat in all forms.

Each meal should be supplemented by 3/4 oz of dried milk, representing a total of 45 grams of protein per week out of the average weekly total of animal protein of 100 grams. In addition, each child was entitled to one-third of a pint of fresh milk every day, providing 30 grams of protein a week.

1964

Uniform arrangements for the remission of charges for school meals on grounds of hardship were introduced, based on national Supplementary Benefit rates.

1965

The report of the Working Party on the Nutritional Standard of the School Dinner, published in 1965, recommended that the overall nutritional standard of the meal should be maintained. This was to maintain a safeguard for children who had to rely heavily on the school meal as a source of protein and other nutrients.

The report recommended that there should be no change to the nutritional value and balance of the school meal, but that a greater variety of meat should be used. Fresh meat should be served on three days a week, and the main dish on the other two days should be built around other food of animal protein origin.

1966

The Department of Education and Science launched a campaign to encourage take-up of school meals, following publication of the *Report on Circumstances of Families* by the Ministry of National Insurance, which indicated that only half the families who qualified for free school meals were taking them.

1967

Full financial responsibility for the school meals service was passed to LEAs, with the introduction of the Rate Support Grant in 1967. This resulted in loss of central control and enabled LEAs to exercise greater discretion over the meals provided and the pricing policy.

1968

As part of its economy measures, the government discontinued the supply of free milk to pupils at secondary schools, and to senior pupils at all-age and middle schools. Only children in primary schools and at special schools continued to receive free milk.

1969

The Provision of Milk and Meals Regulations were updated in 1969, and specified that "on every school day there shall be provided, and on any other day there may be provided, for every pupil as a midday dinner, a meal suitable in all respects as the main meal of the day". The standards intended by the term 'suitable' were specified in the 1965 report on nutritional standards. Other meals and refreshments could be provided as LEAs considered appropriate.

The regulations also introduced automatic entitlement to free school meals for children whose parents were receiving Supplementary Benefit.

1970

The government's White Paper on *New policies for public spending* outlined the aim that "the charge should eventually cover the running cost" of providing the school meal. The White Paper also affected the provision of free school milk in 1971.

1971

The government launched a campaign to encourage take-up of all welfare benefits, including free school meals. Take-up of free school meals increased to almost 80% of those eligible. Amendments to the 1969 Provision of Milk and Meals Regulations also extended the free school meals service to children of parents on Family Income Supplement, as well as those on Supplementary Benefit.

However, the charge for those paying for school meals was increased, following the announcement in the 1970 White Paper.

The Education (Milk) Act (1971) limited the availability of free milk to five to seven year old pupils only. Free milk was no longer available to pupils over seven, except for children under 12 with a certified medical requirement, and all children in special schools. However, the Act also gave LEAs a new power to provide milk to any pupil who paid for it at all LEA primary and secondary schools.

1974

The government's Committee on Medical Aspects of Food Policy published its first report on *Diet and coronary heart disease*.

1975

The report of the Working Party on the Nutritional Aspects of School Meals was launched by the Department of Education and Science and the Welsh Office. The report reviewed the nutritional standards and recommended that the energy and protein recommendations should remain unchanged.

- The average school dinner should provide a minimum of one-third of the recommended daily intake of energy, or 880 calories.
- The meal should continue to provide one-third to half (or 42%) of the recommended daily intake of protein, or 29 grams of protein for an average meal.
- The minimum amount of fat provided by a school dinner should no longer be specified.
- No recommendation was made for the type of fat to be used, but "there are good culinary reasons for using vegetable oils in preference to animal fats for frying".

- There was no longer a standard for animal protein.
- Fresh meat should be served on three days a week, and other animal foods, such as fish, eggs and cheese, should be served on the remaining two days.
- Margarine fortified with vitamin D should be used for school catering.
- The use of milk and cheese should be encouraged in the school dinner, as the richest assimilable sources of calcium.
- Where meals are cooked centrally and distributed in insulated containers, fresh fruit or salads should be served frequently.

In the same year, a report on *Catering in schools*, published by the Department of Education and Science and the Welsh Office, made recommendations for the modification of the Rate Support Grant arrangements for school meals.

1980

The Education Act (1980) is particularly important in the history of school meals, as it removed the obligation on LEAs to provide school meals, except for children entitled to free school meals. The Act also removed the obligation for meals to be sold at a fixed price, and for them to meet any nutritional standards. LEAs were therefore left to decide whether or not they provided meals for the majority of pupils, and the price, type and quality of the meals they did provide. They were still required to provide adequate facilities for children to eat their own packed lunches.

Section 22 of the Act also made discretionary rather than obligatory the provision of free school milk: LEAs were left to decide whether to provide milk at all, and whether to charge for it. Many LEAs decided to discontinue school milk.

In Scotland, similar provisions were made under the 1980 Education (Scotland) Act.

The government stated two reasons for introducing these major changes: financial and innovative. Net expenditure on the school meals service had been rising steadily and was over £400 million per year in England alone. School meals were identified as one area within education where substantial savings in public expenditure could be made with the least effect on education. Secondly, the government accepted that non-traditional forms of provision, notably the cash cafeteria, could give better results than the standard approach of a set menu in terms of efficiency and wastage, and consumer choice and satisfaction.

1982

The Education, Science and Arts Committee recommended a return to nutritional standards for school meals. The government at the time rejected the notion, leaving LEAs to seek guidance if they wished.

1983

A dietary survey of British school children was carried out to assess the impact of the school meals provisions of the Education Act (1980) on the diets of children. The survey was commissioned by the Department of Health and Social Security and the Scottish Home and Health Department in response to a recommendation by the Committee on Medical Aspects of Food Policy's Sub-committee on Nutritional Surveillance (see Chapter 4).

The discussion paper on *Proposals for nutritional guidelines for health education in Britain*, prepared for the National Advisory Committee on Nutrition Education (NACNE), was published. The report recommended reductions in fat, saturated fat, added sugars, salt, and alcohol, and an increase in dietary fibre, and set nutritional goals for the 1980s and for the year 2000.

1984

The Committee on Medical Aspects of Food Policy (COMA) published its report on *Diet and cardiovascular disease*, outlining recommendations for a healthy diet. COMA recommended that fat intakes should be reduced to 35% of food energy; saturated fat should be reduced to 15% of total food energy; intake of sugars should not be increased; consideration should be given to ways of reducing dietary salt intake; and fibre-rich starchy foods should be increased.

1986

The Social Security Act (1986) was passed, limiting the right to free school meals to those children whose parents received Income Support (previously Supplementary Benefit). Children in families receiving Family Credit (previously Family Income Support for low-income families) were no longer eligible, but the family was entitled to a cash amount to compensate for the loss of the free school meal. The power of LEAs to remit the whole or part of the normal charge of school meals was also abolished.

LEAs also lost the power to provide free milk to pupils: only those children from families receiving Income Support remained eligible for free school milk at midday. All other milk had to be charged for.

The initial findings of the government survey on the diets of British school children were published.

1987

The Coronary Prevention Group and Community Nutrition Group of the British Dietetic Association published guidelines for school meals based on a combination of the 1979 Recommended Daily Amounts (RDAs) and the recommendations of NACNE and COMA.

1988

The Social Security Act (1986) came into force in 1988, leading to a reduction in the number of pupils eligible for free school meals.

The Education Reform Act (1988) introduced Local Management of Schools (LMS) and the National Curriculum, both of which have an impact on school meal provision (see Chapter 3).

The enactment of the Local Government Act (1988) introduced compulsory competitive tendering (CCT), obliging all LEAs to put school meals services out to tender. Under this legislation, LEAs are required to draw up specifications for the school meals service and invite bids both from external catering companies and from the internal Direct Service Organisations. While the specification can include 'quality' standards, there is no provision for external monitoring nor mandatory standards under this Act.

1989
The Department of Health published the report of the COMA Panel on Dietary Sugars, which concluded that tooth decay is positively related to the frequency and amount of non-milk extrinsic sugars consumed. Concern was also expressed that sugars might 'dilute' other nutrients in the diet, which may be a problem for people on low food intakes, such as those on slimming diets. The Panel recommended that the consumption of non-milk extrinsic sugars should be decreased, and replaced by fresh fruit, vegetables and starchy foods.

The full report of the government's study of the diets of British school children, carried out in 1983, was published.

1991
The report on Dietary Reference Values, by the Committee on Medical Aspects of Food Policy, was published. This report reviewed the 1979 Recommended Daily Amounts (RDAs) for food energy and nutrients for groups of people in the UK, and gave guidance on Dietary Reference Values for meal provision for energy, macronutrients, vitamins and minerals.

1992
The School Meals Campaign, supported by over 50 national organisations, was launched, and called for the reintroduction of nationally agreed nutritional standards for school meals.

The government's strategy for health in England, *The health of the nation*, was published. As part of the action to achieve the nutrition targets, the government committed itself to producing and disseminating voluntary nutritional guidelines for catering outlets, including the school meal service. The government also committed itself to participation in the World Health Organization 'healthy schools' initiative.

BIBLIOGRAPHY

Department of Education and Science and Welsh Office. 1975. *Catering in schools. Report by the Committee on Catering Arrangements in Schools.* London: HMSO.

Department of Education and Science and Welsh Office. 1975. *Nutrition in schools. Report of the Working Party on the Nutritional Aspects of School Meals.* London: HMSO.

Department of Education and Science. 1982. *School meals. The government response to the seventh report from the Education, Science and Arts Committee. Session 1981-82.* London: HMSO.

Department of Education and Science. 1988. *A short history of the school meals service.* Unpublished paper.

Department of Health and Social Security. 1973. *First report by the Sub-committee on Nutritional Surveillance.* Report on health and social subjects 6. London: HMSO.

Department of Health and Social Security. 1984. *Diet and cardiovascular disease. Committee on Medical Aspects of Food Policy: report of the Panel on Diet in Relation to Cardiovascular Disease.* Report on health and social subjects 28. London: HMSO.

Department of Health and Social Security. 1989. *The diets of British schoolchildren. Sub-committee on Nutritional Surveillance. Committee on Medical Aspects of Food Policy.* Report on health and social subjects 36. London: HMSO.

Department of Health. 1989. *Dietary sugars and human disease. Committee on Medical Aspects of Food Policy: report of the Panel on Dietary Sugars.* Report on health and social subjects 37. London: HMSO.

Department of Health. 1991. *Dietary Reference Values for food energy and nutrients for the United Kingdom. Report of the Panel on Dietary Reference Values of the Committee on Medical Aspects of Food Policy.* Report on health and social subjects 41. London: HMSO.

National Advisory Committee on Nutrition Education (NACNE). 1983. *Proposals for nutritional guidelines for health education in Britain.* London: Health Education Council.

The Coronary Prevention Group and British Dietetic Association. 1987. *Diet or disease? The case for school meals guidelines.* London: The Coronary Prevention Group.

The Food Commission and Child Poverty Action Group. 1991. *School meals fact sheet.* London: Child Poverty Action Group.

White J, Cole-Hamilton I, Dibb S. 1992. *The nutritional case for school meals.* London: School Meals Campaign.

Young I. 1992. *A study of the effects of a school health promotion initiative, relating to healthy eating, on the knowledge, attitudes and behaviour of the pupils.* Masters of Public Health dissertation: University of Glasgow.

CHAPTER 3

The current status of the school meal service

SUMMARY

The majority of schools in the UK provide school meals or some kind of food. Set meals are most common in primary schools, while secondary schools more commonly have a cash cafeteria system.

Uptake of school meals in England fell from 64% of children in 1979, to 42% in 1991, with substantial regional variations. In contrast, in Scotland, uptake of school meals seems to be rising. In 1991, children eating free school meals comprised 28% of all children taking school meals in England. This represents a decrease since 1988, reflecting changes in entitlement criteria.

Since the introduction of compulsory competitive tendering in 1988, all school meals have been put out to tender. Responsibility for the school meals budget currently lies with the local education authority (LEA), although LEAs can choose to devolve the responsibility to individual schools under Local Management of Schools. Many LEAs have tried to improve their school meals service by introducing nutritional guidelines or policies into specifications for contracts. However, few have mandatory nutritional standards, and monitoring of the nutritional content of school meals is very variable. Many LEAs have identified a need for nutritional guidelines for school meals.

School meals are just one important element of the 'health promoting school' – a school which sets a good example, not only through the formal teaching in class but also in the provision of healthy choices in school meals, tuck shops and vending machines. A survey found that a majority of parents thought the priority of the school meal service should be to provide healthy and nutritious meals.

Catering for schools is one of the largest sectors of the UK catering industry, with eight and a half million potential customers every day.

In the 1980s, and particularly since the 1980 Education Act and the 1988 Local Government Act, there have been substantial changes both in the provision of school meals and in patterns of lunchtime eating. Local education authorities (LEAs) have adapted to the situation in a variety of ways[1].

School meals are high on the agenda for any local authority wanting to make cuts. As Simons[2] points out, they are arguably non-essential, non-core activities and, measured against the need to provide children with books and teachers, come low on a local government's priority list for education spending. In a single year, local government expenditure for school meals was cut by 8%, from £380 million in 1990-91 to £350 million in 1991-92.

This chapter examines local authority provision of school meals, trends in the uptake of school meals, and efforts to improve the quality of the meals, including monitoring of their nutritional content. Finally it examines the role of school meals in the context of the 'health promoting school'.

Local authority provision

Since the introduction of the Local Government Act in 1988, all school meals contracts have been put out to tender through compulsory competitive tendering (CCT). The response of local authorities to the changes in legislation has been varied. Some authorities have stopped providing school meals completely, except for those children entitled to free meals, who may simply get sandwiches[3].

The vast majority of school meals contracts are now run by Direct Service Organisations (DSOs): that is, the in-house caterers who ran the service before the introduction of compulsory competitive tendering. Only in very few LEAs is the service run by private caterers and, in a tiny minority, the contracts are divided between the DSO and a private firm. A recent survey commissioned by the Health Education Authority[4] found that in the nine LEAs with a statutory meal service only – that is, provision of free school meals to children whose parents receive Income Support – the DSO only provided packed sandwiches, although many of the schools had made arrangements with private caterers to provide meals*.

The first school meals contracts under CCT were put out to tender in 1989, and the last in 1992. More than two-thirds of these contracts, which tend to be for four years, come up for renewal between July 1993 and September 1995[4].

Provision in schools
The majority of schools still provide school meals or serve some kind of food[6,7]. In general, primary schools have a set meal service, and secondary schools provide a cash cafeteria service.

The Health Education Authority commissioned a survey of English LEAs to review progress on nutritional specifications in school meals contracts. The overall response rate was 87%, giving a representative sample.

Primary schools

In 55% of LEAs in England, primary schools provide a set meal service only, and a further 20% of LEAs also have some schools where there is a cafeteria-style service. On the whole, these cafeterias provide a limited choice of dishes from which the children make up a set-price meal. They are not generally cash cafeterias[4]. In Scotland, by contrast, virtually all primary school catering is now by cash cafeteria.

In 10% of LEAs, primary schools are providing statutory provision only. When only a statutory meal service is offered, most primary schools are unable to provide a hot meal service, and the LEA provides a packed lunch for children entitled to a free meal. If private caterers are providing the food, the LEA normally pays for the 'free meal' children to receive their lunch in the canteen[4].

Recent research by the Consumers' Association found that some of the meals provided in primary schools are 'quite good' from a nutritional point of view. However, meals and menus vary from school to school: some are planned with health and education in mind, while others take a more traditional approach, and include 'children's foods' such as fish fingers and jelly[7].

Secondary schools

In secondary schools, by contrast, cash cafeterias are more popular: in three-quarters (75%) of LEAs, secondary schools provide only a cafeteria service. Secondary schools in less than 2% of LEAs serve only set meals. Cash cafeterias are generally regarded as the only type of food service which is viable in senior schools[4]. The cash cafeteria typically offers a wide variety of snacks and fast food items, as well as home-cooked hot dishes, often as a 'meal of the day', or 'healthy eating choice'.

Less than 2% of LEAs provide, in their secondary schools, a statutory meal service only: most of these provide a cash cafeteria service, using a variety of contractors[4].

The Consumers' Association survey found that school lunches eaten by secondary school pupils tend to be high in fat and sugar, and low in fibre, iron and folate. Children tended to choose the fattier, snack foods[7]. This confirms the earlier findings of the government's survey of the diets of British school children in 1983[5] (see Chapter 4).

Provision for special dietary needs

The vast majority of LEAs make some sort of provision for the needs of vegetarian children, for different ethnic and religious needs and for children with special medical needs[4]. Many LEAs have made a special attempt to meet the specific ethnic needs of children in their schools, and several employ Asian cooks or dining room assistants, buy in specific foods, and have developed special recipes.

However, for caterers the costs are only worth incurring if the school can ensure a sustained demand. In practice, many school children seem to show limited enthusiasm for special ethnic dishes and prefer foods such as fish fingers, beans and chips[4].

Responsibility for managing the school meals budget

The recent introduction of Local Management of Schools (LMS), following the 1988 Education Act, has given schools responsibility for managing their own budgets. The phasing in of LMS began in 1990, and will be complete by 1994. LEAs are not required to devolve responsibility for school meals budgets under LMS, but can choose to do so. It is clear that this legislation could have a further impact on schools catering.

Although it is too early to evaluate the impact of LMS on school meal provision, in some LEAs, responsibility for school catering has already been devolved to schools. The possible effects of LMS on school meals is not currently a major preoccupation for many LEAs[4]. However, in those schools which do take responsibility for school meals under LMS, there are several important practical catering issues, including concerns about equipment, personnel, skills and nutritional expertise, which will affect governors, head teachers and parents.

Uptake of school meals

For more than a decade, the uptake of school meals in England has been declining. In 1979, 64% of children were eating school meals in England. By 1991, this had fallen to 42%[8]. The reduction in the number of children taking school meals was closely associated with the removal, in 1980, of government price controls for school meals. Since April 1988, there has been a further drop, largely attributable to the fall in entitlement to free school meals.

Uptake of school meals varies substantially by region and between schools. Uptake rates appear to be highest in Scotland and the North of England[6]. In 1991, the Local Authority Caterers Association (LACA) found that the uptake in England varied from 67% in the Metropolitan District of Doncaster, to 26% in the London Borough of Enfield[1].

In Scotland, the average uptake of school meals in 1991 was about 50%, representing an increase from about 45% in 1986. Data collected by the Scottish Office Education Department annual census of school meals show a variation between regions from 39% in the Borders, to 70% in Shetland. Free meals in Scotland account for 15-30% of school meals, depending on the region.

Free meal entitlement and uptake

School children qualify for free meals at school if their parents can show evidence that they are in receipt of Income Support. Children who qualify can therefore be taken to be on or below the poverty line[10]. Parents consider free school meals to be an important part of children's diets: they often provide the 'one good meal a day'[11].

TAKE-UP OF FREE AND PAID SCHOOL MEALS IN ENGLAND, 1979-91

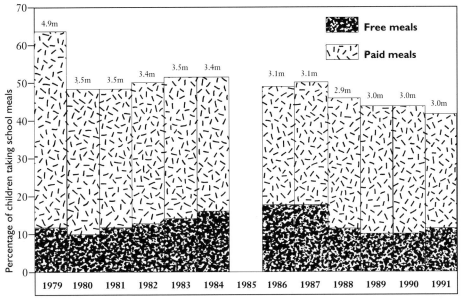

Notes

1   Figures for 1979-88 are from the CIPFA (Chartered Institute of Public Finance and Accountancy) October school meals censuses. These percentages are percentages of the children present in school on the day of the census. No data were collected in 1985. Figures for 1989-91 are from the Department of Education and Science's January censuses. These percentages are the percentages of the total number of children on the school roll.

2   The figures at the top of the columns are the numbers of children eating a school meal on the day of the census.

Source: see reference 9.

The proportion of children taking free school meals rose from 18% in 1979, to 36% in 1987. A change in the entitlement criteria in 1988 led to a drop of 400,000 free school meals, and by 1991, children eating *free* school meals comprised 28% of all children taking school meals in England[8]. The Social Security Act which came into force in 1988 restricted the right to free school meals to those families whose children received Income Support (previously Supplementary Benefit); and families who received Family Credit (previously Family Income Support) were given a cash amount instead[3].

Between 1990 and 1992, the number of children qualifying for free school meals rose, reflecting changing needs and circumstances such as rising levels of unemployment[11,12]. The average percentage of pupils in England entitled to a free meal was 12% in 1991[8], although there is considerable regional variation, ranging from 6% of pupils on the roll in Sutton, to 36% in Westminster[1].

However, not all those entitled to free school meals take them up. In primary schools in England, uptake of free meals was 83%. In secondary schools uptake was 62%[4]. There is also considerable regional variation in those who take up their entitlement to free meals. Take-up may be affected by the stigma of having a free meal[1,12].

Alternatives to school meals

Packed lunches are the most popular alternative among children not eating school meals. The Consumers' Association found that almost half of the children in their study took a packed lunch to school[7]. Typically, a packed lunch included sandwiches, a packet of crisps, a chocolate bar and a sweet drink. They were high in fat and sugar, and low in fibre. Only one in four contained any fruit. Secondary school pupils also bought crisps, chocolate and drinks from the school canteen or vending machine to eat with sandwiches brought from home[7]. This confirms earlier findings from Nottingham, where less than half of the packed lunches included fruit, nearly a third included chocolate, and over two-thirds of children brought crisps[12].

Improving quality

Since the school meals service was put out to competitive tendering in the late 1980s, many LEAs have tried to improve the meals service by introducing nutritional guidelines or policies into contract specifications[4]. Many also have set up initiatives to improve the quality of school meals, and to promote them at a time when the service itself is under threat. These include parent evenings and tasting sessions, healthy eating information and promotions, and healthy tuck shop initiatives[3].

Current use of nutritional guidelines

Since the introduction of the 1980 Education Act, there has been no obligation on LEAs to specify the nutritional content that the school meals must meet. However, among parents in the Consumers' Association's 1992 survey, two-thirds of parents thought that the priority of the school meals service should be to provide healthy and nutritious meals[7].

There have been several attempts to provide nutritional guidelines for school meals since 1980. In particular, health professionals have recognised both the role of childhood diet in health and disease, and the importance of school meals, and have expressed concern about the lack of nutritional standards. In 1987, The Coronary Prevention Group and the British Dietetic Association produced guidelines, and a Private Member's Bill sought, unsuccessfully, to amend the 1980 Education Act to introduce nutritional guidelines for school meals[13,14].

Many LEAs have tried to improve the meals service by introducing such nutritional guidelines. Recent research has indicated, however, that while almost all LEAs claim to have specifications related to healthy eating and nutrition in their contracts for caterers, very few have mandatory standards for nutrients[4].

The responsibility for drawing up the contract specification and for evaluating tenders lies with the 'client' or purchaser side of the school meals organisation, usually the LEA. About two-thirds of LEAs report that they took advice when drawing up the specifications which related to healthy eating and/or nutrition – usually from several sources. Community dietitians were the professionals most commonly consulted for this advice, followed by the local health authority[4]. Several authorities relied on previous nutritional guidelines, as well as the recommendations of the NACNE and COMA reports[15,16].

Many LEAs also have healthy eating guidelines or policies which do not form part of the contract, but which are used to promote good nutrition in school meals. These are usually drawn up with advice from dietitians, local health authorities, or the NACNE and COMA reports, and the great majority have been formally approved by the LEA[4].

Dietitians clearly play an important role in providing advice on nutritional specifications and guidelines for school meals. By the end of 1989, 82% of district health authorities or health boards throughout the UK had a formally approved food and health policy, and these were most frequently coordinated by the dietitian. Over 66% included work on school meals, and 38% on tuck shops[17].

A majority of LEAs have identified the development of nutritional standards for the school meals service as an important need[4]. There is general consensus that government guidance on nutrition for school meals would add weight to LEA attempts to achieve healthy eating.

However, healthy eating may not currently be a priority for the school meals organisation in many LEAs. Although many healthy eating initiatives were carried out in the late 1980s, the major preoccupations in the early 1990s are with the promotion of the service in order to maintain uptake, and with financial viability[1]. Financial concerns, and advice about implementing nutritional standards within budgetary constraints, have been identified as important issues[4].

Current use of nutritional specifications in school meals contracts

In a survey of 109 English LEAs commissioned by the Health Education Authority, Coles and Turner[4] examined contract specifications relating to healthy eating and nutrition provided by 58 LEAs. Seventy of the 109 LEAs provided information on guidelines or policies, although these were not always included in the contract specifications.

Specifications

The recommendations of NACNE[15] and COMA[16] formed the basis of policy or guidelines in two-thirds (66%) of the specifications examined. Recommendations were made for foods, nutrient composition, recipes and cooking methods. However, only 5% of these LEAs specified that the recommendations should be implemented. A quarter (26%) of the documents only listed general healthy eating aims and objectives, and very rarely (2%) were a fixed timescale and quantified objectives included, or were the objectives made mandatory.

Policies

The majority of documents examined (62%) included either a specific or a general healthy eating policy. The implementation of a healthy eating policy was mandatory in only 10% of these, although it was not clear by what criteria the requirements were to be monitored or assessed.

Guidelines

Nutritional guidelines were given by almost half (45%) of LEAs responding, but implementation of the guidelines was mandatory in only about a third of these. There was much variation in the guidelines: some were minimal, while others gave specific quantified recommendations for a range of nutrients. Where LEAs gave detailed guidelines, they tended to reflect the Coronary Prevention Group/British Dietetic Association guidelines, which are based on a combination of the 1979 Recommended Daily Amounts (RDAs) and the NACNE and COMA reports[13,15,16].

Standards

Very few LEAs made nutritional standards mandatory in their specifications – possibly because of difficulties in enforcement and monitoring. However, many of those with mandatory components in their specifications reported no difficulty in meeting them. Although some of the specifications were sufficiently detailed to aid the implementation of healthy eating policies, very few gave any practical recommendations about how they were to be achieved.

Pricing policies

Pricing can clearly have an important impact on the uptake of school meals and of particular items, and some caterers have begun to use pricing policies to increase the take-up of particular healthy choices.

There is considerable variation in the prices charged for school meals. In 1991-92, the price of a set meal ranged from 45p to £1.00 in primary schools[4], and from 70p to £1.18 in secondary schools[1]. The authorised spend, that is the amount of money received by children qualifying for a free school meal in secondary schools, ranged from 55p to £1.41. The prices charged for specific items of food and drink also showed considerable variation. Milk, for example, costs anything between 4p and 30p, and juice between 13p and 34p; chips were priced between 17p and 55p a portion, and jacket potatoes between 11p and 60p[1].

The high rate of EC subsidy on whole milk, whole milk yoghurts, and full-fat cheeses for schools makes it uneconomical tò provide lower fat choices in schools. For example, the subsidy on milk is approximately £1.19 per gallon for whole milk, compared to 75p per gallon for semi-skimmed milk[18]. In 1990-91, semi-skimmed milk contributed only 9% of the milk provided to schools[19].

Monitoring the nutritional content of school meals

Monitoring of contracts is an important part of compulsory competitive tendering, and the majority of LEAs can impose financial penalties for poor performance. However, monitoring may well be constrained by the small number of monitors. Although most authorities employ contract monitors, most monitors have to cover more than 50 schools[1].

Much of the monitoring of school meals concerns hygiene, and health and safety, rather than nutrition, reflecting the enforceable requirements of health and safety legislation[1,4].

Almost all the LEAs whose contracts include nutritional specifications report that these are monitored. However, there is considerable variation in the way in which the monitoring is done, and the extent to which it covers the specifications adequately. Very few LEAs employ a nutritionist as part of the 'client' or purchaser team[4].

The most common methods of monitoring are to check that the menus, ingredients, foods on offer, and portion sizes are as specified in the contract. Ingredients and bought-in products are also commonly checked to ensure that they meet the nutritional requirements. However, less than a quarter of respondents in Coles and Turner's survey reported checking portion sizes, and fewer mentioned checking that standard recipes and cooking methods were followed[4].

Nutritional analysis was used by only a quarter of LEAs who responded. This usually involved the analysis of standard recipes, and then checking compliance with the menu: only in a very few cases were sample meals analysed in a laboratory[4]. There may be difficulties in analysing recipes used in school catering: external analysis can be very costly, and the effective use of data in food tables requires professional expertise and is very time-consuming[18]. The School Meals Assessment Project, a simple computer-based nutritional assessment method being developed by the National Forum for Coronary Heart Disease Prevention, may increase the number of LEAs undertaking analysis.

In 1992, less than 20% of LEAs responding to the HEA survey reported any difficulties in meeting the contract specifications relating to healthy eating, although this may reflect the permissive rather than mandatory nature of the nutrition specifications[4]. A more detailed analysis in a small number of schools found that the specifications for nutrients were met in most cases, although the percentage of energy provided by fat tended to be in excess of the recommendations, and carbohydrate was correspondingly low. Iron and fibre were lower than required in some schools[20].

Although there is scant information on whether the pre-1980 nutritional standards were met, studies in the 1970s highlighted the variations in standards and adequacy of school meals, many of which did not meet the standards set by the Department of Education and Science[21]. In a small survey of schools in 1977, failure to meet nutritional standards seemed to result from inadequate food purchases, poor menu planning and portion control, and several management problems[22]. The same factors could be important considerations today (see also page 47).

Training of caterers

The training of caterers, serving staff and supervisors is an important consideration in improving the nutritional quality of school meals. About two-thirds (62%) of LEAs report that they have encouraged caterers to provide training in healthy eating and nutrition for their staff, and 44% report that their caterers had provided such training during 1991[4].

However, the 1990 Food Safety Act was the most common subject of training provided in 1990-91, by some 90-95% of authorities responding to the LACA survey[1], reflecting the statutory requirement. Health and safety, and food production, were the second most common areas of training covered. For 1992, the areas most commonly identified for training included financial planning, leadership, and staffing and recruitment, reflecting the current preoccupations of caterers, LEAs and schools.

Coles and Turner have suggested that, while nutrition was a focus for training in the late-1980s, there may be less perceived need for it in the early 90s[4].

School meals in the context of the 'health promoting school'

A 'health promoting school' is a school which plays a major role in promoting better health by setting a good example. This means not just covering formal classroom teaching on health-related subjects, but also addressing the 'hidden curriculum' of powerful influences on health.

In terms of healthy eating, the hidden curriculum includes not only the provision of healthy school meals, but also the availability of healthy choices in tuck shops and vending machines. Provision of food in and around the school environment can have an important impact on children's nutrition education and on what children eat during the school day[23].

As part of its strategy for promoting health, the UK government has recently made a commitment to the WHO initiative on the 'health promoting school'[24].

Tuck shops, vending machines and vans

Many schools have tuck shops and vending machines, and some allow access to vans selling snacks in school grounds. However, the majority of LEAs in England have no formal policy governing the food that is sold on the school premises, nor on whether healthier snacks or fruit are sold in tuck shops or machines[4]. In the absence of a formal LEA policy, the decision or policy tends to be made by the head teacher, who decides whether or not vans are allowed in the school, and what food can be sold.

Schools are specifically targeted by soft drinks, confectionery and snack manufacturers, and offered attractive incentives to sell the products. For example, vending machines in schools are often provided rent free, and any profit contributes towards school funds or sports activities. But often the school has to use the vendor's supplies, which may not include a choice of healthier snacks[6].

Research by Gardner Merchant found that crisps, snacks, sweets, and hot snacks are sold in almost nine out of ten schools[6]. Over half of all children buy food at school more than once a week, with one in five buying it almost every day. Crisps are the most common 'extra' bought in schools. The Consumers' Association found that a quarter of secondary school children had two or more packets of crisps in a day, and nearly half had two or more chocolate bars or sweets[6].

The importance of the school meal service

School catering can make an important contribution to children's diets. For some children, the school meal provides the main meal of the day, particularly among those who are entitled to free meals.

A study in 1981 found that 5% of children surveyed had nothing to eat for breakfast and ate only one meal throughout the rest of the day[25]. More recently, a study in 1991 found that almost one in ten secondary school children had nothing to eat before leaving for school in the morning: older girls were the least likely to eat breakfast[6]. The same study found that one in six does not have a hot meal cooked at home in the evening.

Public support for the school meals service was confirmed by the Consumers' Association survey in 1992: nine out of ten parents surveyed thought that it is important for schools to provide school meals[7].

REFERENCES

1   Local Authority Caterers Association. 1991. *Education catering survey 1991.* Compiled by AVL Consultancy Ltd. Middlesex: AVL.

2   Simons C, Sutton A. 1992. School meals rule. In: *Hospitality*: May 1992; 129: 9-16.

3   O'Rourke J, Dibb S, Heughan A. 1992. *School meals fact sheet 1.* London: School Meals Campaign.

4   Coles A, Turner S. 1992. *Catering for healthy eating in schools.* Research carried out for the Health Education Authority. London: Institute of Education/Health Education Authority. In press.

5   Department of Health and Social Security. 1989. *The diets of British schoolchildren. Sub-committee on Nutritional Surveillance. Committee on Medical Aspects of Food Policy.* Report on health and social subjects 36. London: HMSO.

6   Gardner Merchant. 1991. *School meals survey: 'What today's children are eating'.* Prepared by Burson Marsteller.

7   Consumers' Association. 1992. School dinners: are they worth having? In *Which?*; September 1992: 502-504.

8   Department of Education and Science. 1992. *Statistics of education: schools 1991.* London: HMSO.

9   Cole-Hamilton I, Dibb S, O'Rourke J. 1991. *School meals fact sheet.* London: The Food Commission and Child Poverty Action Group.

10 Lane MG. 1992. Free school meals. In: *Society of Public Health: Faculty of Community Health Newsletter;* iv: II: p7.

11 McEvaddy S. 1988. *One good meal a day – the loss of free school meals.* London: Child Poverty Action Group.

12 White J, Cole-Hamilton, Dibb S. 1992. *The nutritional case for school meals.* London: School Meals Campaign.

13 The Coronary Prevention Group and British Dietetic Association. 1987. *Diet or disease? The case for school meals guidelines.* London: The Coronary Prevention Group.

14 Proposed *Education (Nutritional Requirements) Bill, 1987. A Bill to amend the 1980 Education Act to make provision with respect to nutritional requirements for school meals and for connected purposes.*

15 National Advisory Committee on Nutrition Education (NACNE). 1983. *Proposals for nutritional guidelines for health education in Britain.* London: Health Education Council.

16 Department of Health and Social Security. 1984. *Diet and cardiovascular disease. Committee on Medical Aspects of Food Policy: report of the Panel on Diet in Relation to Cardiovascular Disease.* Report on health and social subjects 28. London: HMSO.

17 Gibson L, Kallevik J. 1990. *Food health policies: the UK district health authority and health board national survey: progress report.* London: Health Education Authority.

18 Intervention Board. 1990. *School milk subsidy.* Leaflet number LP20 (p17, Annex II, issued July 1991). Reading: Intervention Board.

19 Nurick J (ed). 1992. School milk: Britain is number two. *Food and Drink Parliamentary Monitor;* 67: 9.

20 Bonner G. 1992. *A descriptive study of the way in which contract specifications affect the nutritional content of school meals.* BSc project thesis: The Polytechnic of North London. Unpublished.

21 Cook J, Altman DG, Jacoby A et al. 1975. School meals and nutrition of schoolchildren. *British Journal of Preventive and Social Medicine;* 29: 182.

22 Bender AE, Harris MC, Getreuer A. 1977. Feeding of school children in a London borough. *British Medical Journal;* 1: 757-759.

23 Young I. 1992. *A study of the effects of a school health promotion initiative, relating to healthy eating, on the knowledge, attitudes and behaviour of the pupils.* Masters of Public Health dissertation: University of Glasgow.

24 Department of Health. 1992. *The health of the nation: a strategy for health in England.* London: HMSO.

25 National Dairy Council. 1981. *What are children eating these days?* London: National Dairy Council.

CHAPTER 4

The nutritional content of children's diets

SUMMARY

The diets of children in Britain tend to be high in fat, high in sugar, low in non-starch polysaccharides (fibre), low in iron and calcium, and possibly low in folate.

School meals make an important contribution to the daily diets of school children – particularly those from low-income families – contributing between 30-43% of children's average daily energy intake.

Although school meals do not meet all the recommended amounts of nutrients and tend to provide a high percentage of energy from fat, they may represent the best option when compared to other sources of food available to children for the midday meal: for example packed lunches, or meals bought in cafes or take-aways.

If the aim is to reduce the burden of preventable disease for the next generation, there is a need for a more nutrient-rich diet for children, with particular emphasis on calcium, iron, non-starch polysaccharides, and the micronutrients from fruit and vegetables. School meals could make an important contribution.

In the 1980s and early 90s, concerns about the nutritional content of children's diets have centred not so much on under-nutrition, but on the possibility that the dietary habits of school children, and their continuation into adulthood, may contribute to the development of dental caries, anaemia, obesity and later diseases such as coronary heart disease, osteoporosis and certain forms of cancer. The high consumption of fatty and sugary foods, the low consumption of fruit and vegetables, and the resulting low intakes of iron and calcium, give particular cause for concern.

Throughout the 20th century, school meals have made an important contribution to the diets of school children. They represent a vital opportunity to provide food that is nutritious and wholesome, to address some of the concerns about children's current and future health, and to educate children about a healthy diet.

What are children eating today?

The government's report, *The diets of British schoolchildren*[1], provides a benchmark for information on children's diets. The survey provides comprehensive data on the food and nutrient intake of over 2,500 children aged 10/11 and 14/15 in 1983. It was commissioned by the Department of Health and Social Security (DHSS) in order to monitor the effects of the 1980 Education Act on children's diet, including changes in provision and the removal of nutritional standards for school meals.

Developments since the DHSS survey include the NACNE report[2], the COMA (Committee on Medical Aspects of Food Policy) report on diet and cardiovascular disease[3], and the COMA report on dietary sugars and human disease[4]. These reports, which make recommendations for a healthy diet, have stimulated a range of healthy eating initiatives both in schools and in the wider environment.

Several smaller studies of children's diets have been carried out since the 1983 DHSS survey. The overall conclusion is that the nutritional content of children's diets has not improved over the 1980s and early 90s, even though the food sources may be very different.

DHSS survey, 1983: *The diets of British schoolchildren*

The 1983 survey of school children's diets[1] found that the majority of British school children were exceeding the recommendation for fat intake and that some groups of children failed to meet the recommended daily intake of one or more micronutrients.

The nutrient intakes of the children were compared with the Recommended Daily Amounts (RDAs) set by COMA in 1979[5]. The survey found that:

- On average, children were consuming 90% of the recommended energy, although this did not in itself seem to be inadequate in relation to growth.
- The average proportion of energy from fat ranged from 37.4% to 38.7% in the different age and sex groups. Three-quarters of children had intakes of fat above COMA's 1984 recommendation of 35% of energy. Milk and chips were the main single sources of fat.
- The average intakes of protein, thiamin, nicotinic acid and vitamin C were above the RDA in all age and sex groups.
- Among girls, the average intakes of iron were below the RDA.
- Intakes of riboflavin (vitamin B2) were below the RDA among older girls. Compared to other children, this group was eating less milk and breakfast cereals – the major sources of this vitamin.
- Although average intakes of calcium in older girls were close to the RDA, almost 60% of older girls consumed less than the RDA. This reflected a lower consumption of the main dietary sources of calcium, namely milk, bread and other cereals.

- Primary school children in Scotland had lower average intakes of vitamin A precursors and vitamin C than children in other parts of Britain, reflecting a lower consumption of carrots and other vegetables.
- Children receiving free school meals had poorer diets overall, and were particularly dependent on their school meals to provide vitamin C.

The main single sources of dietary energy in the children's diets were bread, chips, milk, biscuits, meat products, cake and puddings. Chips and milk intake were the main items in the diet which varied with social class. Children in manual social classes were more likely to eat chips and less likely to drink milk.

Further analyses of the survey showed generally low consumption of other micronutrients such as retinol, vitamin B6, vitamin E, folate, magnesium and zinc[6].

Since the survey was carried out, the Recommended Daily Amounts (RDAs) have been revised[7]. A more recent comparison of the data with the government's 1991 Dietary Reference Values (DRVs) has indicated that as many as one in three girls may have iron intakes below the Lower Reference Nutrient Intake (LRNI) and one in four may have similarly low calcium intakes[8].

Other surveys of British children's diets

Several smaller studies on children's diets carried out since 1983 have confirmed the findings of the DHSS survey[1]. They indicate that children are still not getting adequate amounts of some micronutrients such as iron and calcium and, despite health education recommendations and advice, are still eating diets high in fat and sugar, and low in fruit and vegetables.

Diets of younger children

There are few data on dietary intake among very young school children. However, Whincup[9] collected dietary information among 3,000 children aged five to seven, using a 24-hour dietary recall, in 1987-88. The study found very marked social class and regional variation in food consumption, with children in manual social groups and those in the North eating less fruit and vegetables than those in non-manual groups and those in the South. The findings were consistent with social and regional variations in adult intakes of fruit and vegetables. Similar patterns were found in a 1990 study of five to seven year olds using a food frequency questionnaire[10].

In a study of 227 children aged 7-10 and 11-12 years in 1988, in Kent and north London, Nelson[11] reported similar findings to those of the 1983 DHSS survey. The study, in which the children weighed and recorded all food and drink consumed in one week, found that the intakes of boys were greater than those of girls for all nutrients, except copper and vitamin C in the younger age group, and for all the nutrients except vitamins A, C and E in the older children. The heights and weights of the children were similar to those found in the DHSS survey[1].

Table 2 — DAILY NUTRIENT INTAKES: BOYS 10-14 YEARS

		RDA*	DRV (RNI)[7]	DHSS[1]	Nelson et al[11]	McNeill et al[14]	Hackett et al[16]	Adamson et al[15]
Year of report/study		1979	1991	1983	1988	1988/89	1980	1990
Age of children		10-11 years	11-14 years	10-11 years	11-12 years	12 years	11-12 years	11-12 years
ENERGY	MJ	9.68◆	9.27	8.67	7.74	8.96	8.90	8.61
	kcal	2,316	2,220	2,074	1,852	2,144	2,129	2,060
FAT	g (% energy)	80◆	(35%)†	88 (37%)	(38%)	93 (39%)	95 (39%)	91 (39%)
STARCH	g (% energy)	295◆	(39%)**†	—	—	163	152	146
TOTAL SUGAR	g (% energy)	43◆	—	274 (51%)	—	117	119 (22%)	118 (22%)
NME SUGARS	(% energy)	—	(11%)†	}	—	—	(15%)	(17%)
FIBRE	g	25◆	18 (NSP)	—	17	16	—	9 (NSP)
PROTEIN	g	66	42	61	61	61	61	62
IRON	mg	12	11	10	11	10	10	12
CALCIUM	mg	700	1000	833	768	822	850	786
ZINC	mg	15●	9	—	8	8	—	—
MAGNESIUM	mg	350●	280	—	—	232	—	—
PHOSPHORUS	g	1.2●	0.8	—	—	1.1	—	—
VITAMIN A ***	μg	725	600	854	685	494	527****	552****
VITAMIN B1 (thiamin)	mg	1.1	0.9	1.2	1.2	1.2	—	—
VITAMIN B2 (riboflavin)	mg	1.4	1.2	1.7	1.6	1.5	—	—
VITAMIN B3 ※	mg	16	15	27	—	27	—	—
VITAMIN B6 (pyridoxine)	mg	1.6●	1.2	1.2	1.3	1.1	—	—
VITAMIN B12	μg	2.0▲	1.2	—	3.3	2.8	—	—
FOLATE ■	μg	300	200	—	155	105	—	—
VITAMIN C	mg	25	35	49	67	47	38	52
VITAMIN D	μg	2.5▲	—	1.5	1.7	2.0	1.9	2.4
VITAMIN E	mg	8●	—	—	4.5	4.8	—	—

Code and sources for Tables 2 and 3
*   Includes other recommendations (see below)
***   DRV for starch and intrinsic and milk sugars
****   Median retinol equivalent intakes
◆   Retinol equivalents
●▲※   Food and Agriculture Organisation/World Health Organization/United Nations University (1985)
■   Total folate
( )   % of total energy
†   % of food energy

Source: See references 1, 5, 7, 11, 14, 15, 16.

Table 3

DAILY NUTRIENT INTAKES: GIRLS 10-14 YEARS

		RDA*	DRV (RNI)[7]	DHSS[1]	Nelson et al[11]	McNeill et al[14]	Hackett et al[16]	Adamson et al[15]
Year of report/study		1979	1991	1983	1988	1988/89	1980	1990
Age of children		10-11 years	11-14 years	10-11 years	11-12 years	12 years	11-12 years	11-12 years
ENERGY	MJ	8.60●	7.72	7.69	7.45	8.14	8.27	8.25
	kcal	2,057	1,845	1,840	1,782	1,947	1,980	1,974
FAT	g/(% energy)	70◆	(35%)†	79 (38%)	(38%)	85 (39%)	90 (40%)	89 (40%)
STARCH	g	262◆	(39%)***†	—	—	143	137	133
TOTAL SUGAR	g (% energy)	38◆	—	}241 (49%)	—	110	115 (22%)	119 (23%)
NME SUGARS	(% energy)	—	(11%)†		—	—	(16%)	(18%)
FIBRE	g	25◆	15 (NSP)	—	17	15	—	9 (NSP)
PROTEIN	g	53	41	53	57	55	54	57
IRON	mg	12	15	9	10	10	9	11
CALCIUM	mg	700	800	702	701	767	751	763
ZINC	mg	15●	9	—	7	7	—	—
MAGNESIUM	mg	300●	280	—	—	205	—	—
PHOSPHORUS	g	1.2	0.6	—	—	—	—	—
VITAMIN A ***	µg	725	600	691	718	510	471****	585****
VITAMIN B1 (thiamin)	mg	0.9	0.7	1.0	1.0	1.0	—	—
VITAMIN B2 (riboflavin)	mg	1.4	1.1	1.4	1.3	1.4	—	—
VITAMIN B3 ✳	mg	16	12	23	—	24	—	—
VITAMIN B6 (pyridoxine)	mg	1.6●	1.0	1.0	1.2	1.0	—	—
VITAMIN B12	µg	2▲	1	—	3	3	—	—
FOLATE ■	µg	300	200	—	141	90	—	—
VITAMIN C	mg	25	35	49	68	28	38	56
VITAMIN D	µg	2.5▲	—	1.3	1.5	1.8	1.9	2.4
VITAMIN E	mg	8●	—	—	4.7	4.8	—	—

Abbreviations for Tables 2 and 3
DHSS — Department of Health and Social Security
DRV — Dietary Reference Values
NSP — Non-starch polysaccharides
NME SUGARS — Non-milk extrinsic sugars
RDA — Recommended Daily Amounts
RNI — Reference Nutrient Intake

Source: See references 1, 5, 7, 11, 14, 15, 16.

Among the 11-12 year olds[12], average nutrient intakes were substantially above the Recommended Daily Amounts (RDAs) for all nutrients except energy, iron and vitamin D. However, there was no deficit in growth, and the low energy intakes were consistent with a generally sedentary lifestyle.

A comparison of these data with the government's most recent nutrition recommendations (Reference Nutrient Intakes: RNIs) showed that the average intakes for younger children were at or above the RNI for all nutrients except energy[13]. Older children, aged 11-12 years, were above the RNI for all nutrients except energy, iron and calcium.

Sugar and fat intakes increased with increasing energy intake, but there was no change in the proportion of energy derived from sugar in any of the groups, and only a small, statistically non-significant rise in the percentage of energy from fat. As Nelson points out[12], this suggests that the higher intakes were derived from eating more of the same type of diet, rather than a different diet, richer in fatty or sugary foods.

The Nelson study found no difference in body mass index (BMI) between the different energy groups among the 11-12 year olds[12]. This suggests that differences in energy intake were associated with differences in levels of activity.

The dietary intake of secondary school children in Dundee was assessed by McNeill in 1988[14]. Sixty-one 12 year old children recorded and weighed their food intake for one week. The study found that intakes of fat and sugar were high, and intakes of starch and fibre were low. All reflect the intakes recorded in several adult studies. The proportion of energy derived from fat (39%) was similar to that among the children in the 1983 DHSS survey[1].

The overall nutrient intakes of the children in Dundee were very similar to those among the children in the DHSS survey, although the Dundee girls had a slightly higher calcium intake, and both boys and girls in Dundee had a lower vitamin A and higher vitamin D intake. As McNeill[14] points out, the lower vitamin A intake may reflect the fact that the school was in a lower income area of Dundee: data for the UK as a whole show lower intakes of vitamin A in lower socioeconomic groups[1].

A comparison of these data with the newer Dietary Reference Values shows that, on average, children failed to meet the Reference Nutrient Intake (RNI) for iron, calcium, vitamin A and folate, zinc and magnesium (see Tables 2 and 3).

More recently, Adamson et al[15] collected data on children's food intakes from sources both inside and outside the home. Almost 400 children aged 11-12 completed two three-day food diaries, each followed by a 20-minute interview. The results showed that, on average, 40% of energy was provided by fat, 48% by carbohydrate (including 22% of total energy from total sugars), and protein contributed 12%.

The proportion of energy derived from fat had not changed since a study carried out in the same schools 10 years earlier in 1980 by Hackett et al[16], and the results support earlier findings by the DHSS[1] that more than three-quarters of children ate over 35% of their energy as fat.

In keeping with earlier studies, Adamson et al[15,17] found that average calcium and iron intakes were lower than the recommended values (see Tables 2 and 3). For calcium intake, 83% of boys and 66% of girls fell below the Reference Nutrient Intake (RNI). Furthermore, 90% of girls fell below the RNI for iron.

Diets of older children and adolescents

In a study of 4,760 teenagers aged 16 and 17 years, using a four-day dietary diary in 1986-87, Crawley[18] found intakes of macronutrients similar to those found in other studies of a similar age group. Intakes of fat and extrinsic sugars were substantially above the Dietary Reference Value (DRV) recommendations of 35% and 11% respectively, and intakes of intrinsic sugars, milk sugars and starch and non-starch polysaccharides (NSP) were lower than the DRV recommendations.

The average fat intake among the teenagers was 42% of total energy – higher than that found by the DHSS[1] among 14-15 year olds (39%) and by Gregory[19] among 16-24 year olds (38%), but similar to that reported by Bull[20] among 15-18 year olds (43%). Much of the fat in the diet was derived from meat and meat products, and milk and milk products, suggesting that the diet of these adolescents was also high in saturated fat. However, achieving less than 33% energy from fat was associated with an increase in the intake of non-milk extrinsic sugars and alcohol.

The adult DRV of 18g per day of NSP was achieved by only a quarter (25%) of boys and one in ten (10%) of girls. A significant number of teenagers (13% of boys and 30% of girls) achieved only half the recommended intake.

The results indicate that few 16-17 year olds achieve the DRVs for energy, macronutrients and NSP. This confirms the findings of the DHSS[1] and Gregory[19]. In a separate analysis of vitamin and mineral intakes of these 4,760 teenagers, Crawley[21] found that the intakes of all vitamins and minerals were sufficient, except iron and riboflavin (vitamin B2) in girls, confirming previous estimates by the DHSS[1]. However, girls who were eating low-energy diets had low intakes of vitamin A, riboflavin (B2), vitamin B6, and calcium and iron.

Thus, although most teenagers have diets that provide more than the recommended amount of most vitamins, intakes of iron and riboflavin are low for most girls, and girls on low-energy diets are consuming intakes of vitamins and minerals below the recommended amounts. Although these need further investigation, Crawley[21] points out that they do not necessarily reflect nutrient deficiencies, as the recommended amounts give a wide safety margin.

In a study of over 900 15-25 year olds in 1982, using a two-week diary, Bull[20] found the following:

15-18 year old boys
— Average energy intake was only 84% of the recommended level.
— Average fat intake was 42% of energy.

— Intakes of iron and thiamin (vitamin B1) were lower than the recommended level.
— Among all the 15-25 year old males in the study, the 15-18 year old group had the lowest intake of protein, nicotinic acid, vitamin B12, and folic acid.

15-18 year old girls
— Average energy intake was only 86% of the recommended amount.
— Average fat intake was 43% of energy.
— Average iron intake was only 71% of the recommended level.
— Average riboflavin (vitamin B2) intake was marginally below the recommended level.
— Among all the 15-25 year old females in the study, the 15-18 year old group had the greatest average intake of carbohydrate.

There was a social class gradient in average nutrient intakes, which were lower among young adults in social groups D and E than among those in groups A and B. Among young men, those in social groups D and E had the lowest average intakes of thiamin (vitamin B1), riboflavin (vitamin B2), vitamin C and calcium. Among young women, those in groups D and E had the lowest average intakes of energy, protein, calcium, thiamin (vitamin B1), riboflavin (vitamin B2), nicotinic acid and fat.

The contribution of school meals

The 1983 DHSS survey[1] illustrated the relative importance of school meals to the daily diets of children, particularly those from low-income families. School meals may be especially important for those who do not eat breakfast, or do not eat supper. For some children, the midday meal is the only substantial meal they eat all day.

Several studies have examined the contribution made by school meals to children's nutritional intake.

School meals before the 1980 Education Act

Nelson and Paul[22] studied the food intake of 191 primary and secondary school children in Cambridge aged 5 to 17, using seven-day diaries of measured food consumption in 1977-79. The data provide a baseline against which the changes in children's diets following implementation of the 1980 legislation on school meals can be assessed.

The study found that school meals contributed less than one quarter of what was then the Recommended Daily Amount (RDA) for energy, iron, and riboflavin (vitamin B2), and less than a third of the RDA for protein, calcium, thiamin (vitamin B1) and vitamin C. School dinners provided a smaller proportion of a day's nutrient intake than did other midday meals, such as packed lunches or lunches eaten at home, for all nutrients except protein and vitamin C. However, total average energy intake was lower on school-dinner days than other weekdays.

Nelson and Paul's study also indicated that school meals did not meet the nutritional standards set by the Department of Education and Science (DES) in 1975. The nutritional targets set down for school meals in 1975 were 33% of the RDA for energy, and 42% of the RDA for protein. On average, the meals eaten provided only about three-quarters of these targets – that is, 24% and 32% of the RDAs respectively. The findings confirm those of earlier studies[23,24,25].

The data from Nelson and Paul's study indicate that the school meals fell short of the target for two reasons. Firstly, the portions requested and eaten by the children were smaller than those recommended. Secondly, the analysed nutrient content of many school foods was less than the published value in the food tables used for menu-planning[22], largely due to the higher moisture content and consequent dilution of nutrients in the school foods. This latter finding confirmed earlier studies[23,25] (see also page 35).

Only cooked meals at home achieved the DES targets for energy and protein intakes for midday meals, showing that the targets can be attained. However, as Nelson and Paul[22] point out, it may have been unrealistic to expect routine catering in schools to achieve the standards reached by home cooking.

Richardson and Lawson[25] had earlier pointed out that, although the quality and size of school meals did not meet DES targets, they nevertheless represented the best value for money in comparison to other midday sources of food.

An earlier study, carried out by Cook between 1968 and 1970[26] found that children taking school meals had a higher lunchtime nutrient intake than children not taking school meals, and that school meals provided a higher proportion of daily nutrient intake than other meals. It also found that school meals provided a higher proportion of daily intake for children from social classes IV and V compared to intakes for other social classes.

School meals after the 1980 Education Act

The 1983 DHSS study on the diets of British school children concluded that dietary patterns of food consumed were to some extent dependent on the provision of school meals. On average, school meals contributed between 30% and 43% of the average daily energy intake of children. In terms of the average energy or nutrient intake, there was no difference between children taking school meals in cash cafeterias and those eating a set-price, fixed menu meal[1].

Although the total average daily intakes of energy and nutrients did not vary with the kind of meal eaten on weekday lunchtimes, school meals contributed over half the chips consumed by older children and over half the buns and pastries eaten by younger children in the survey.

The overall diet was poorest in older children, particularly those who ate lunch out of school at places such as cafes, or take-away or fast food outlets. Their lunchtime meals tended to be low in many nutrients, and particularly iron, and this was not compensated for in other parts of their diet. The school meal made a particularly important contribution to the energy content of the diets of older children[1].

More recently, in 1992, Adamson et al[17] found that, among 11-12 year olds, school meals were the single largest source of food energy obtained from outside the home, and contributed about half of the total food energy consumed outside the home. School meals were high in fat and vitamin C, reflecting a high consumption of chips and fruit juice.

When lunchtime food sources – including school meals, home lunches (including packed lunches), and other food sources (shops/take-aways) – were compared[27], school meals provided the greatest amount of protein, calcium, iron and vitamin C (see Table 4). However, they also provided a high percentage of energy from fat (43%), which was the same as that provided by the lunches from home. School meals were also lower in sugars than other food sources, but non-milk extrinsic sugars still contributed 11.7% of the total energy in the meals: more than the recommended maximum amount.

The lunches bought from shops/take-aways offered the poorest option for nutritional content: they were the lowest source of protein, calcium, iron and vitamin A (retinol equivalents), and were the highest in non-milk extrinsic sugars (18% of total energy).

Although school meals may not meet all the recommended amounts of nutrients, they may represent the best option when compared to other sources of food available to children for the midday meal. A re-analysis of the DHSS survey data[8] and more recent research by Adamson et al[27] showed that, on the whole, school meals provided higher levels of vitamins and minerals than either packed lunches or meals bought in a cafe or take-away. There is some indication that primary school meals may be nutritionally better than meals eaten in secondary schools[28].

Children in low-income families
Several studies have indicated that school meals play a particularly important role for children from low-income families.

The 1983 DHSS survey found that children receiving free school meals had lower average intakes of vitamin A and C. However, the school meal made a relatively high contribution to their overall vitamin C intake in particular, indicating that the overall nutrient intake for this group depended more on school meals than did that of more affluent children.

Nelson and Paul[22], in 1979, found that children from lower income families received a significantly higher proportion of the day's nutrient intake from school meals. Parents in lower income groups were often not providing another cooked meal in the evening, and thus school meals provided an essential contribution to the energy and nutrient intakes of those children whose home diets were, on average, less than adequate[20].

Children from lower income families had larger school meals, and obtained

Table 4	AVERAGE NUTRIENT INTAKE PER MEAL FROM SCHOOLDAY LUNCHTIME FOOD SOURCES

Northumbrian boys and girls aged 11–12 years in 1990

Place of purchase (number of subjects)	ENERGY MJ kcal	FAT g (% energy)	CARBOHYDRATE g (% energy)	NME SUGARS g (% energy)	UNAVAILABLE CARBOHYDRATE g	NSP g	PROTEIN g (% energy)	IRON mg	CALCIUM mg	VITAMIN A (retinol equivalents) µg	VITAMIN C mg
SCHOOL LUNCH (n=279)	3.04 728	35.0 (42.8)	88.5 (45.9)	22.3 (11.7)	4.5	2.7	19.7 (11.3)	3.81	283.9	183.5	24.7
SHOP/TAKEAWAY LUNCH (n=53)	3.05 729	30.7 (38.4)	105.6 (54.3)	34.2 (18.0)	5.4	2.0	13.5 (7.3)	2.95	144.1	48.1	14.1
HOME LUNCH including packed lunches (n=177)	2.45 586	28.7 (42.6)	69.8 (45.3)	21.8 (14.2)	5.3	3.2	17.5 (12.1)	3.05	211.5	178.4	14.1

Abbreviations
NME SUGARS   Non-milk extrinsic sugars
NSP   Non-starch polysaccharides

Source: See reference 27.

a larger proportion of their daily nutrient intake from school dinners than children from higher income families. The study indicated that school meals were most important nutritionally for lower income families[22].

Poor growth has also been found in children receiving free school meals, that is, children in low-income families, and nutritional support outside the home for children from lower income families may therefore be important[29,30].

Conclusion

Although the energy content of children's diets has been falling over several decades as children become less physically active, they require a proportionally greater nutrient intake than adults, and therefore a more nutrient-dense diet. Children's intakes of several nutrients give cause for concern, both for short and long-term health (see Chapter 5).

The studies outlined in this chapter confirm that the diets of school children in Britain tend to be high in fat, high in sugars, low in non-starch polysaccharides, and low in iron and calcium:

- Children's diets are high in fat, and over the 1980s and early 90s there has been no significant change in the proportion of energy derived from fat, despite nutritional recommendations and advice.
- The consumption of added sugar among children is high and has not fallen over the 1980s and early 90s. Some research suggests it may have increased slightly[31].
- Children's consumption of fruit and vegetables, and their intake of non-starch polysaccharides, are low and seem to reflect adult social class and regional variations.
- Low iron intakes among children give cause for concern, particularly among adolescent girls.
- Calcium intakes are relatively low among school children, particularly among boys. Dietary calcium in childhood and adolescence may be particularly important for the accumulation of bone mass.
- Folate intakes appear to be lower than the recommended intakes, and this may be particularly important for adolescent girls.
- Slimming is common among teenagers. Among girls on low-energy diets, there may be a particular problem with low intakes of calcium and iron, and vitamin A, vitamin B2 (riboflavin) and vitamin B6.
- Children in low-income families have particularly low intakes of several nutrients. Nelson has pointed out that the diets of children from low-income families may need to be of a higher quality than the diets of children in higher social classes, in order to confer the same nutritional benefit[32].
- Low vitamin D intakes cause concern only among populations with limited exposure to sunlight. Nelson[11] suggests that as long as outdoor activity is a normal part of the school curriculum, it is unlikely that pupils would have inadequate tissue levels of vitamin D.

While it is possible that some of the reported low intakes of iron and calcium may be due to methodological bias, these findings do give cause for concern. Intakes of some other nutrients may not be low enough to show symptoms of deficiency, but it has been suggested that they may be at a level which is below that needed for optimal physical and mental performance, although this is contentious[12]. Chapters 5 and 6 give further details of the health consequences of low levels of different nutrients, and Appendix 3 gives details of rich sources of nutrients.

The nutrient intake of children may not be very different from that of children in previous decades and the quality is similar to that of the present day adult population, although the foods from which these nutrients are derived may be very different[14]. The trend towards more food being eaten away from the home seen in the general population is also reflected in the diets of children, and food eaten outside the home is an important source of energy[17].

School meals can contribute to a healthy diet, and represent a better source of nutrients for children at lunchtime than do cafes, shops or other food outlets. The Consumers' Association survey[28] has indicated that the nutrient composition of school meals in primary schools (primarily set meals) may be better than that of meals in secondary schools (primarily cash cafeterias). However, since 1980, with increased prices of school meals, the trend has been towards more children bringing packed lunches or going to local cafes or take-aways.

School milk could also make an important contribution to the calcium content of children's diets. Milk is an important source of calcium: in 1983, it contributed at least 30% of the calcium in children's diets. The loss of free school milk for many children since 1986 may have had an impact on calcium intakes[13].

If the aim is to reduce the burden of preventable disease for the next generation, there is an urgent need for a more nutrient-rich diet for children, with particular emphasis on calcium, iron, non-starch polysaccharides and the micronutrients from fruit and vegetables. School meals can make an important contribution to such a diet.

REFERENCES

1   Department of Health and Social Security. 1989. *The diets of British schoolchildren. Sub-committee on Nutritional Surveillance. Committee on Medical Aspects of Food Policy.* Report on health and social subjects 36. London: HMSO.

2   National Advisory Committee on Nutrition Education (NACNE). 1983. *Proposals for nutritional guidelines for health education in Britain.* London: Health Education Council.

3   Department of Health and Social Security. 1984. *Diet and cardiovascular disease. Committee on Medical Aspects of Food Policy: report of the Panel on Diet in Relation to Cardiovascular Disease.* Report on health and social subjects 28. London: HMSO.

4   Department of Health. 1989. *Dietary sugars and human disease. Committee on Medical Aspects of Food Policy: report of the Panel on Dietary Sugars.* Report on health and social subjects 37. London: HMSO.

5   Department of Health and Social Security. 1979. *Recommended Daily Amounts of food energy and nutrients for groups of people in the United Kingdom.* Report on health and social subjects 15. London: HMSO.

6   Doyle W. 1986. Analyses carried out at the Nuffield Laboratory of Comparative Medicine, Institute of Zoology. Unpublished data.

7   Department of Health. 1991. *Dietary Reference Values for food energy and nutrients for the United Kingdom. Report of the Panel on Dietary Reference Values of the Committee on Medical Aspects of Food Policy.* Report on health and social subjects 41. London: HMSO.

8   The Food Commission. 1991. School meals best source of nutrients. *The Food Magazine*; 15: 2: 20.

9   Whincup P. 1992. Personal communication.

10   Whincup P. 1992. Personal communication.

11   Nelson M, Naismith DJ, Burley V, Gatenby S, Geddes N. 1990. Nutrient intakes, vitamin supplementation and intelligence in British schoolchildren. *British Journal of Nutrition*; 64: 13-22.

12   Nelson M. 1991. Food, vitamins and IQ. In: *Proceedings of the Nutrition Society*; 50: 29-35.

13   White J, Cole-Hamilton I, Dibb S. 1992. *The nutritional case for school meals.* London: School Meals Campaign.

14   McNeill G, Davidson L, Morrison DC, Crombie IK, Keighran J, Todman J. 1991. Nutrient intake in schoolchildren: some practical considerations. *Proceedings of the Nutrition Society*; 50: 37-43.

15   Adamson A, Rugg-Gunn AJ, Butler T, Appleton DR, Hackett A. 1992. Nutritional intake, height and weight of 11 to 12 year old Northumbrian children in 1990 compared with information obtained in 1980. *British Journal of Nutrition*; 68: 3.

16   Hackett A, Rugg-Gunn AJ, Appleton DR, Eastre JE, Jenkins GN. 1984. A two-year longitudinal nutritional survey of 405 Northumberland children initially aged 11.5 years. *British Journal of Nutrition*; 51: 67-75.

17   Adamson A, Rugg-Gunn AJ, Butler T, Appleton DR. 1992. The place of purchase of food in the diets of 11 to 12-year old adolescents. Poster presentation at British Dietetic Association.

18   Crawley H. 1992. The energy, nutrient and food intakes of teenagers aged 16/17 years in Britain: i. energy, macronutrients and non-starch polysaccharides. *Proceedings of the Nutrition Society.* In press.

19   Gregory J, Foster K, Tyler H, Wiseman M. 1990. *The dietary and nutritional survey of British adults.* London: HMSO.

20   Bull N. 1985. Dietary habits of 15 to 25-year olds. In: *Human Nutrition: Applied Nutrition*; vol 39A: supplement 1: 1-68.

21   Crawley H. 1991. The vitamin and mineral intakes of teenagers aged 16/17 years in Britain. Paper prepared for Booker Nutritional Products.

22   Nelson M, Paul A. 1983. The nutritive contribution of school dinners and other mid-day meals to the diets of schoolchildren. In: *Human Nutrition: Applied Nutrition*; 37A: 128-135.

23   Bender AE, Harris MC, Getrueur A. 1977. Feeding of schoolchildren in a London borough. *British Medical Journal*; 1: 757-759.

24   McAllister A, Hughes J, Jones M. 1981. A study of junior school meals in South Glamorgan. *Journal of Human Nutrition*; 35: 369-374.

25 Richardson DP, Lawson M. 1972. Nutritional value of midday meals of senior schoolchildren. *British Medical Journal*; 4: 697-699.

26 Cook J, Altman DG, Jacoby A, Holland WW, Elliot A. 1975. School meals and the nutrition of schoolchildren. *British Journal of Preventive and Social Medicine*; 29: 182-189.

27 Adamson A, Rugg-Gunn AJ, Butler T, Appleton DR. 1992. Unpublished data.

28 Consumers' Association. 1992. School dinners: are they worth having? *Which?*; September 1992: 502-504.

29 Rona RJ, Chinn S, Smith AM. 1979. Height of children receiving free school meals. *Lancet*: 2: 534.

30 Baker IA, Elwood PC, Sweetman PM. 1979. Free school meals and height of Welsh schoolchildren. *Lancet*; 2: 692.

31 Rugg-Gunn AJ, Hackett AF, Jenkins GN, Appleton DR. 1991. Empty calories? Nutrient intake in relation to sugar intake in English adolescents. *Journal of Human Nutrition and Dietetics*; 4: 2: 101-111.

32 Nelson M, Paul AA. 1981. Socio-economic influences of nutrient intake in children. In: Turner M (ed). *Preventive nutrition and society:* 121-130. London: Academic Press.

CHAPTER 5

The health implications of children's diets

SUMMARY

Diet in childhood is particularly important for three reasons. Firstly, children need a nutrient-dense diet to meet their requirements for growth and development. Secondly, health-related behaviour and attitudes towards food are established in childhood. Thirdly, while some diet-related diseases manifest themselves in childhood, there is good evidence that the disease process for some diseases of adulthood may start in early life.

Children's diets may contribute to a variety of health problems both in childhood and in later life. As well as affecting children's growth and development, diet in childhood may also contribute to: dental disease, nutritional anaemia, obesity and overweight, low bone mass, coronary heart disease, stroke, certain forms of cancer, and possibly reduced mental performance in undernourished children.

There are substantial health benefits in a diet that is low in fat and sugar, and high in starchy foods, with plenty of fruit and vegetables, both in the short and the long term.

The contribution of diet to health is well recognised. Medical and scientific research has established clear links between dietary factors and the risk of developing coronary heart disease, hypertension, stroke, some kinds of cancer, anaemia, dental disease, obesity, diabetes, osteoporosis, and other chronic diseases[1]. On the basis of the current evidence, the UK government has set targets for reducing ill health and deaths from diet-related causes[2].

Diet in childhood is particularly important, for several reasons[3,4,5]:

- As children are growing, they have an increased requirement for nutrients relative to their body weight. Children's diets therefore need to be of high quality – that is, of high nutrient density.
- Health-related behaviour patterns and attitudes towards food are acquired and established in childhood. If children adopt healthy eating

patterns, it is likely that they will maintain these habits into adulthood.

● Some diet-related diseases are manifested in childhood. There is good evidence that the disease processes for other diseases of adulthood may also start in early life.

This chapter outlines the major health problems to which children's diet may contribute, both in childhood and in later life.

Growth and development

Growth and stature are common measures of overall nutritional status. The need for nutrients in childhood is also closely related to the speed of growth. Children require a proportionally greater nutrient intake than adults, and therefore need to eat a more nutrient-dense diet[4].

Over time, there has been a trend towards taller children in the UK. There is a strong relationship between growth and social class: children of lower income families tend to have lower energy intakes, and tend to be shorter. The National Study of Health and Growth found that children's height is most influenced by their parents' height, although several environmental factors, including diet, are also important. Children from low-income families, who were entitled to free school meals, tended to be shorter[6].

Dental disease

Dental decay is one of the most common childhood diseases in the UK: more than 50% of children have tooth decay before their second set of teeth appear. Dental caries can occur at any age, but those at greatest risk include children and adolescents[7].

Sugars are the most important dietary cause of dental caries. The development of tooth decay is positively related to the amount and frequency of 'added' or non-milk extrinsic sugars consumed in the diet[7]. The correlation is most marked when sugar is eaten both between meals and at meals[8].

For example, a clear relationship has been found between annual sugar consumption and the incidence of dental caries among Japanese school children[8]. In a review of studies from 11 European countries covering 750,000 children, reductions were seen in both the prevalence and the severity of caries in all studies carried out during the second World War, when sugar intakes fell[8].

A World Health Organization report suggests that the development of caries is more directly related to the *frequency of consumption* of sugary foods rather than to the *total consumption* of sugars[9]. A higher caries incidence has been associated with frequent intake of buns and cakes with meals, and confectionery[10], the availability of sweets at school canteens[11], and the sale of biscuits in school canteens[12].

There is no clinical reason why dental decay in children should not be virtually eliminated[13]. The risk of caries can also be reduced by non-dietary means, particularly the use of fluoride[7]: increased use of fluoride is responsible for the decline in caries incidence in many groups over recent years. However, the COMA Panel on Dietary Sugars has pointed out that, if the prevalence of dental caries in the UK is to be reduced further, it will be necessary to reduce the amount and frequency of consumption of non-milk extrinsic sugars[14].

Nutritional anaemia

Anaemia is one of the most common diet-related deficiency diseases. Iron deficiency is the main cause of anaemia, although folic acid deficiency and vitamin B12 deficiency may sometimes be important. Young children and adolescents are particularly vulnerable to iron deficiency, due to their high physiological requirements to meet tissue growth[15]. Iron deficiency is most prevalent between the age of six months and two years. Anaemia may also be a problem for adolescents, when there is an increased need for iron during the growth spurt. Adolescent girls are at particular risk, because of menstruation, and low iron intake among girls in the UK seems to be a problem.

In a study of almost 400 middle-class London children aged 12-14 in 1990, Nelson[16] found that the prevalence of anaemia was 14.5% in the group with iron intakes less than the LRNI (Lower Reference Nutrient Intake) and low vitamin C intakes. Anaemia was three times more common in girls than boys, and was particularly common among girls who reported that they had tried to lose weight over the past year (23%), and among vegetarians (25%).

The government's report on Dietary Reference Values also points to high levels of anaemia in Asian children, possibly due to late weaning and inappropriate foods[15]. In a study of about 80 Asian girls aged 12-15 years, Nelson[17] found that 16% were anaemic.

Symptoms of anaemia include general fatigue and lassitude, giddiness, and breathlessness on exertion. The functional effects of iron deficiency also include adverse effects on intellectual performance and behaviour[15]: iron deficiency anaemia has been associated with low scores on tests of development, learning and school achievement[18,19].

As people become less active, they may eat less food and thereby reduce their total iron intake. A reduction in fat and sugar intakes and their replacement with nutrient-dense foods could lead to a reduction in anaemia[8].

Mental performance

There has been much concern about whether diet can affect intellectual performance, and particularly about effects on children who miss breakfast[20]. Research suggests that cognitive functions are more vulnerable in poorly nourished children[21]. However Nelson concludes that, among the majority of British children, there is no evidence that learning ability or mental performance is limited by the quality of the diet[22,23]. However, there is significant concern that deficiencies may be important for a small minority of children in the UK who have sub-clinical vitamin and mineral deficiencies[24]. The issue remains controversial, particularly since reliable research among children is most difficult in the more deprived groups who are theoretically most likely to have problems.

Obesity and overweight

Obesity and overweight are now a major nutritional problem among both adults and children in the UK. A national survey of primary school children in the early 1980s found that 8% of boys and 10% of girls were obese when measured by triceps skinfold thickness, and at age 11, 10% of boys and 13% of girls were obese[25].

The number of overweight and obese adults in the UK is increasing, and although there are little reliable data for children, it is likely that the same trend is occurring[26]. Adamson and Rugg-Gunn[27], for example, found that in two small samples of about 400 children aged 11-12 years, examined 10 years apart in 1980 and 1990, the mean Body Mass Index (BMI) rose by 0.41 in boys and 0.30 in girls. The prevalence of obesity (a BMI of over 25) between the samples doubled over this 10-year period, from 2% to 4%. However, the validity of the BMI in children has been questioned.

Obesity has both genetic and environmental causes. It results from a higher energy intake than is needed to balance energy expenditure, and so is related to both diet and physical activity. However, a diet rich in energy-dense foods, containing a lot of sugar and fat, seems to be particularly conducive to the development of obesity. Research suggests that the BMI in children and adults may be related to the proportion of energy derived from dietary fats, irrespective of other factors[28].

In adulthood, obesity has been linked to an increased risk of stroke, coronary heart disease, high blood pressure, high blood cholesterol, non-insulin dependent diabetes, gall bladder disease, osteoarthritis, and certain types of cancer. It may also aggravate other health problems[29,30]. Obese children also have higher blood cholesterol and blood pressure levels in comparison to their lighter weight peers[3].

There is some debate about how well obesity 'tracks' into adulthood: that is the extent to which obese children become obese adults. The Bogalusa Heart Study in the US found that height and weight tracked particularly well among children, over eight years of follow-up[3].

The Royal College of Physicians has concluded that there is little doubt that overweight children are at an increased risk of becoming overweight adults[31]. The risk of being overweight in adulthood is related to the degree of overweight in childhood. Being overweight at age 13 is a fairly strong predictor of adult weight problems[32,33].

However, many normal weight children will also become overweight by middle age, due to a cumulative excess of energy intake over energy expenditure, which points to the need for emphasising good nutritional and exercise habits for all children. Garrow has pointed out that the opportunities for primary prevention of obesity are chiefly with school children aged 7-12[32,33]. A reduction in non-milk extrinsic sugars and in fats, as part of a general reduction in energy intake, are important in both the prevention and treatment of obesity[7,29,30,31].

Diabetes

The risk of non-insulin dependent diabetes mellitus – in terms of both onset and severity – is strongly associated with both the duration and level of obesity[8]. In the UK, diabetes (both non-insulin dependent and insulin dependent diabetes) affects about 500,000 people. The prevalence of non-insulin dependent diabetes is almost five times higher among populations of Asian origin than among those of UK origin.

Slimming diets

Dieting is also an important health problem in adolescence, particularly since teenagers on slimming diets are more likely to be short of essential vitamins and minerals than children on higher energy diets. Furthermore, the intake of sugars may 'dilute' other nutrients in the diet among people who are on low-energy diets, including slimmers.

The government's survey of British school children found that 8% of 14-15 year old girls claimed they were on a diet to lose weight[34]. More recently, in a survey of 16-19 year olds, the Health Education Authority found that over half of all girls interviewed had been on a diet to lose weight at some stage, compared to 16% of boys, and almost a quarter of girls were on a diet at the time of the survey[35]. Lawson[4] suggests that up to 80% of girls diet or indulge in 'binge' eating at some stage, and in a small minority, this persists and progresses.

Bone mass

Over the last century, the major metabolic bone problem in northern Europe has changed from rickets and osteomalacia, to osteoporosis and a consequent epidemic of fractures in older people.

About 45% of the total adult skeletal mass is laid down during adolescence. The accumulation of substantial bone mass during childhood and early adult life helps to prevent the total bone mass from falling to a critical level later in life[8].

Throughout life, physical activity and a good supply of dietary calcium are both important to the accumulation and maintenance of bone mass. It seems likely that there is a relationship between dietary calcium intake in childhood and adolescence and peak bone mass in middle age[36]. The highest requirements for calcium are during infancy and adolescence, followed by childhood and early adulthood. However, average calcium intakes tend to be low among teenagers and young adults, and this may limit bone growth and affect adult height or lead to lower bone densities.

In a review, Boyle has concluded that there is great scope for addressing the increasing problem of post-menopausal bone fractures through increased dietary calcium in childhood, and increased physical activity at all ages[36], although the optimal intakes of calcium in relation to maximising bone mass have yet to be determined.

Rickets, which results from prolonged deficiency of vitamin D, continues to be a problem among the Asian population, although the incidence has been falling since the early 1980s[36]. It is possible that this has been helped by fortification of foods with vitamin D. Low vitamin D status is relatively common among Asians in the UK, particularly among children and adolescents. The type of vegetarian diet, a low intake of calcium, and limited exposure to sunlight all contribute to this problem[15].

Coronary heart disease

Coronary heart disease (CHD) is the major cause of death in the UK, including deaths under the age of 65. The major known risk factors include raised blood cholesterol, hypertension and smoking.

There is little doubt that the disease process begins in childhood: cardiovascular risk factors can be identified in early life, and lifestyles and behaviours which influence cardiovascular risk are learned and begin early[37,38]. The prevalence of obesity, blood pressure and blood cholesterol varies from one child population to another, as does the incidence of cardiovascular disease in adult populations. Furthermore, there is evidence that weight, blood cholesterol levels and blood pressure levels 'track' from childhood into adult life: that is, they tend to remain in a given rank relative to the child's peers[3].

The World Health Organization[39] concludes that, since risk factors found in childhood are potentially predictive of adult CHD, efforts to prevent the disease should begin in children.

Serum cholesterol

The link between the development of CHD and the level of total blood cholesterol is well established: in population studies, the risk of CHD rises with increasing blood cholesterol levels.

It is now well recognised that atherosclerosis can begin early in life. Fatty streaks, some of which may be precursors of atherosclerotic plaques, are found in the aortas of children as young as three years, and appear in the coronary arteries during the second decade of life. Autopsies on young American soldiers who died in the Korean and Vietnam wars found more advanced atherosclerotic lesions in many of the young adults[38]. Evidence from the Bogalusa Heart Study shows that the extent of fatty streaks in the aorta is very strongly related to the levels of total blood cholesterol in very young children[3].

On a population level, there are large differences in the average serum cholesterol level of children that correlate well with the average for the adult population, and with adult rates of CHD[38].

On an individual level, evidence from four major studies in the US shows that cholesterol levels tend to 'track' during childhood, and the rank a child holds for total cholesterol at a young age tends to be maintained relative to his or her peers, and tracks throughout adolescence into adulthood[40]. Thus children with raised blood cholesterol levels will become adults with raised cholesterol levels, and will be at increased risk of later CHD.

The major non-genetic determinant of blood cholesterol is diet, and particularly intakes of saturated and polyunsaturated fatty acids. An increase in the intake of some types of dietary fibre also leads to a fall in serum cholesterol[8].

There is also strong evidence for the importance of dietary and other factors in determining blood cholesterol levels in childhood. International comparisons show large differences between the serum cholesterol levels of children living, for example, on a diet low in total and saturated fat, and children living on a diet which is high in fat and particularly saturated fat[38]. Cholesterol levels are correlated with saturated fat consumption and body weight[41]. Infants with persistently high intakes of saturated fat have been found to have higher concentrations of total blood cholesterol at all ages between four and seven years[3].

A reduction in consumption of saturated fat lowers serum cholesterol levels in children. For example, in the North Karelia project, dietary intervention aimed at children through a nutrition programme in schools and a community-wide approach resulted in a significant reduction in serum cholesterol levels[40].

Other dietary factors

The government's report on Dietary Reference Values[15] notes the increasing evidence that increased intakes of antioxidants such as beta-carotene, and vitamins C and E, found primarily in fresh fruits and vegetables, may protect against conditions such as CHD and cancer. Some of the benefits of a high-fibre diet, rich in vegetables and cereals, may also relate to its other effects, such as a lowering in blood pressure[8].

Stroke

Stroke is a major cause of disability in the UK, and accounts for over 10% of all deaths. The principal risk factor for stroke is high blood pressure, which is also important in the development of coronary heart disease.

Hypertension

There are indications that adult hypertension may be determined during childhood, but the precise factors occurring during childhood that predict adult hypertension are not well defined[42]. In the US, the Bogalusa and Muscatine studies have found that many children have blood pressure levels that are considered high by adult standards. Blood pressure appears to 'track' with time less consistently than serum cholesterol levels, but evidence suggests that children with abnormally high blood pressure levels are more likely to become hypertensive adults, with an increased cardiovascular disease risk[43].

Although many factors contribute to the development of hypertension, obesity and the consumption of salt seem to be particularly important[8]. For many years, it has been recognised that a low-salt diet can be important in the treatment of hypertension. While the role of salt in the causation of hypertension remains to some extent controversial, the World Health Organization[44] has advised that, on the basis of existing evidence, salt intake should be reduced.

Prospective and intervention studies have included an analysis of the effects of salt on blood pressure in children. Blood pressures in babies fed a low-sodium diet for the first six months of life were, on average, 2mmHg lower than those of babies fed a normal-sodium diet, and significant differences in the rate of increase in blood pressure from birth were found[8].

The World Health Organization[42] has concluded that the prevention of high blood pressure in childhood and adolescence is important for the prevention of hypertension in adult life: the earlier prevention starts, the more likely it is to be effective. Furthermore, the habits associated with an undue rise in blood pressure with age are formed early, and become increasingly difficult to change later in life.

The government's report on Dietary Reference Values points out that physiological requirements for sodium are low, and current sodium intakes needlessly high[15]. Reductions in sodium intake, early prevention of obesity, and increased physical activity during childhood may have a large impact on the occurrence of essential hypertension[42].

Cancer

Cancer accounts for almost a quarter of all deaths in the UK. In 1991, the government's Chief Medical Officer suggested that 20-60% of all cancers may be linked with dietary factors, with a best estimate of 35%[45]. The diet suggested for the prevention of CHD is also likely to reduce the risk of cancer: a diet relatively low in fat and rich in vegetables and fruit is associated with a lower risk of a variety of cancers, including those of the breast and bowel[2]. However, while little is known so far about the links between childhood diet and adult cancer, healthy eating habits established in childhood will help to reduce the risk of cancer later in life.

Breast cancer

It is widely acknowledged that dietary fat may be important in the development of breast cancer[15]. It has been suggested that saturated fatty acids play an important role in the development of breast cancer, and other associated dietary factors, including overweight, may also prove to be important[8].

Colon cancer

A positive correlation has been shown between colon cancer and total fat intake, and between colon cancer and meat consumption, in cross-country studies[46]. However, other studies have not shown a consistent association[15].

There is some debate about the protective nature of dietary fibre in the development of colon cancer. Most epidemiological studies show an apparent protective effect of dietary fibre against colon cancer, although there are confounding factors arising from the lower fat and animal protein intakes of high-fibre diets. There are also independent protective effects associated with the consumption of fruit and vegetables[8].

REFERENCES

1   Cannon G. 1992. *Food and health: the experts agree*. London: Consumers' Association.
2   Department of Health. 1992. *The health of the nation: a strategy for health in England*. London: HMSO.
3   Berenson GS, Srinivasan SR, Webber LS et al. 1991. *Cardiovascular risk in early life: the Bogalusa Heart Study*. Michigan: The Upjohn Company.
4   Lawson M. 1992. Nutrition in childhood. In: *Nutrition, social status and health: proceedings of a conference*. London: National Dairy Council.
5   Boulton TJC. 1985. Patterns of food intake in childhood and adolescence and risk of later disease. *Australian and New Zealand Journal of Medicine*; 15: 478.
6   Rona RJ, Chinn S, Holland WW. 1988. The national study of health and growth. In Department of Health Report on health and social subjects 33: *Third report of the Sub-committee on Nutritional Surveillance, Committee on Medical Aspects of Food Policy*. London: HMSO.
7   Health Education Authority. 1990. *Sugars in the diet. Briefing paper*. (A briefing paper based on the Report of the COMA Panel on Dietary Sugars, *Dietary Sugars and Human Disease*.) London: Health Education Authority.
8   James WPT. 1988. *Healthy nutrition: preventing nutrition-related diseases in Europe*. WHO Regional Publications, European Series, No. 24. Copenhagen: World Health Organization Regional Office for Europe.
9   World Health Organization. 1984. *Prevention methods and programmes for oral diseases. Report of a WHO Expert Committee*. WHO Technical Report Series, No. 713. Geneva: World Health Organization.
10 Bjarnason S, Finnbogason SY, Noren JG. 1989. Sugar consumption and caries experience in 12- and 13-year-old Icelandic children. *Acta Odontol Scand*; 47: 315-321.
11 Fanning EA, Gotjamanos T, Vowles NJ. 1969. Dental caries in children related to availability of sweets at school canteens. *The Medical Journal of Australia*; i: 1131-1132.
12 Pengelly JPB, Brist U, Smyth JFA. 1972. Incisor caries and primary school tuckshops. *Public Health, London*; 86: 183-188.

13 Department of Health. 1991. *The health of the nation: a consultative document for health in England.* London: HMSO.

14 Department of Health. 1989. *Dietary sugars and human disease. Committee on Medical Aspects of Food Policy. Report of the Panel on Dietary Sugars.* Report on health and social subjects 37. London: HMSO.

15 Department of Health. 1991. *Dietary Reference Values for food energy and nutrients for the United Kingdom. Report of the Panel on Dietary Reference Values of the Committee on Medical Aspects of Food Policy.* Report on health and social subjects 41. London: HMSO.

16 Nelson M, White J, Rhodes C. 1992. Haemoglobin, ferritin and iron intakes in British children aged 12-14 years: a preliminary investigation. *British Journal of Nutrition.* In press.

17 Nelson M. 1992. Personal communication.

18 Pollitt E et al. 1985. Cognitive effects of iron deficiency anaemia. *Lancet*; i: 85.

19 Deinhart AS et al. 1986. Cognitive deficits in iron deficient anaemic children. *Journal of Paediatrics*; 108: 681-689.

20 Dickie NH, Bender AE. 1982. Breakfast and performance in schoolchildren. *British Journal of Nutrition*; 48: 483-496.

21 Simeon DT, Grantham-McGregor S. 1989. Effects of missing breakfast on the cognitive functions of school children of differing nutritional status. *American Journal of Clinical Nutrition*; 49: 646-653.

22 Nelson M, Naismith DJ, Burley V et al. 1990. Nutrient intakes, vitamin-mineral supplementation, and intelligence in British schoolchildren. *British Journal of Nutrition*; 64: 13-22.

23 Nelson M. 1991. Food, vitamins and IQ. *Proceedings of the Nutrition Society*; 50: 29-35.

24 Addy DP. 1986. Happiness is: iron. *British Medical Journal*; 292: 969-970.

25 Rona RJ, Chinn S. 1984. The national survey of health and growth: nutritional surveillance of primary school children from 1972-1981 with special reference to unemployment and social class. *Annals of Human Biology*; 11: 17-28.

26 Gregory J, Foster K, Tyler H, Wiseman M. 1990. *The dietary and nutritional survey of British adults.* London: HMSO.

27 Adamson A, Rugg-Gunn AJ, Butler T, Appleton DR, Hackett A. 1992. Nutritional intake, height and weight of 11 to 12 year old Northumbrian children in 1990 compared with information obtained in 1980. *British Journal of Nutrition*; 68: 3.

28 Lean MEJ, James WPT, Garthwaite PH. 1989. Obesity without overeating. In: Bjorntorp P, Rossner S (eds): *Obesity in Europe 88*, pp 281-286. London: John Libbey.

29 Garrow JS. 1992. Treatment of obesity. *Lancet*; 340: 409-413.

30 Ravussin E, Swinburn BA. 1992. Pathophysiology of obesity. *Lancet*; 340: 404-408.

31 Black D, James WPT, Besser GM et al. 1983. *Obesity: a report of the Royal College of Physicians.* London: Royal College of Physicians.

32 Garrow JS. 1988. *Obesity and related diseases.* Edinburgh: Churchill Livingstone.

33 Garrow JS. 1991. *Obesity and overweight. Briefing paper for the Health Education Authority.* London: Health Education Authority.

34 Department of Health. 1989. *The diets of British schoolchildren. Sub-committee on Nutritional Surveillance. Committee on Medical Aspects of Food Policy.* Report on health and social subjects 36. London: HMSO.

35 Health Education Authority. 1990. *Young adults' health and lifestyles: diet.* Research conducted by MORI on behalf of the Health Education Authority. London: Health Education Authority.

36 Boyle IT. 1991. Bones for the future. *Acta Paediatr. Scand.*; supplement: 373: 58-65.

37 Lewis B. 1988. Diet and coronary heart disease: implications for childhood nutrition. In: *Should the prevention of coronary heart disease begin in childhood?* Report of a conference. London: The Coronary Prevention Group.

38 Wynder E. 1988. Coronary heart disease prevention: should it begin in childhood? In: *Should the prevention of coronary heart disease begin in childhood?* Report of a conference. London: The Coronary Prevention Group.

39 World Health Organization. 1990. *Prevention in childhood and youth of adult cardiovascular disease: time for action.* Geneva: World Health Organization.

40 American Health Foundation. 1983. Conference on blood lipids in children: optimal levels for early prevention of coronary artery disease. Epidemiological section. *Preventive Medicine;* 12: 741-797.

41 Ward SD, Melin JR, Lloyd FP et al. 1980. Determinants of plasma cholesterol in children – a familial study. *American Journal of Clinical Nutrition;* 33: 63-70.

42 World Health Organization Study Group. 1985. *Blood pressure studies in children: report of a WHO study group.* WHO Technical Report Series 715. Geneva: World Health Organization.

43 Lauer RM, Connor WE, Leaverton PE et al. 1975. Coronary heart disease risk factors in school children: the Muscatine study. *Journal of Paediatrics;* 86: 697-706.

44 World Health Organization. 1983. *Primary prevention of essential hypertension: report of a World Health Organization scientific group.* WHO Technical Report Series 686. Geneva: World Health Organization.

45 Acheson D. 1991. *On the state of the public health: annual report of the Chief Medical Officer.* London: HMSO.

46 Armstrong B, Doll R. 1975. Environmental factors and cancer incidence in different countries with special reference to dietary practices. *International Journal of Cancer;* 15: 617-631.

CHAPTER 6

Nutritional guidelines for school meals

Nutritional standards for school meals were set by the Department of Education and Science until the 1980 Education Act. Since then, local education authorities (LEAs) have been left to determine their own nutritional standards for the school meals service.

Policies and guidelines used by LEAs since 1980 tend to reflect the broad nutritional recommendations of NACNE[1] and COMA[2]. Many of the more detailed nutritional guidelines currently in use are based on the guidelines produced by The Coronary Prevention Group and the British Dietetic Association[3]. These were based on a combination of the government's 1979 Recommended Daily Amounts (RDAs) of food energy and nutrients for groups of people in the UK[4], and the NACNE and COMA reports.

This chapter outlines the nutritional guidelines for school meals proposed by The Caroline Walker Trust Expert Working Group on Nutritional Guidelines for School Meals.

Dietary Reference Values

In 1991, the government published revised quantified nutritional guidelines for the nation, in the form of Dietary Reference Values (DRVs)[5]. These differ from the 1979 RDAs in several ways. The range of nutrients has been extended from 10 to 34. The Reference Nutrient Intakes (RNI), which inform the school meals guidelines presented here, represent the amount of nutrient sufficient for almost all individuals in a group. The nearest equivalent to the RNI is the 1969 Recommended Daily Intake – that is the amount sufficient or more than sufficient to meet the nutritional needs of practically all healthy individuals in a population. If the average intake of a group is at the RNI, then the risk of deficiency in the group is very small.

The RNI is appropriate for planning food supplies for groups, including institutional catering such as school meals. Energy, however, is expressed as an Estimated Average Requirement (EAR): that is the average requirement of a group for energy. About half the group will usually need more than the EAR, and half will need less.

The figures provided by the government's report on Dietary Reference

Values are intended to provide guidance on appropriate dietary composition and meal provision. The recommendations have been made on the basis of current evidence on the physiological needs and the health effects of diet, and pragmatic judgement. As there is no absolute requirement for fats, sugars or starches (except essential fatty acids), the Panel on Dietary Reference Values made pragmatic judgements for these nutrients based on the changes in physiological or health outcomes which would be expected to result from changes in current intakes. The DRVs for fat and carbohydrate are based on studies among adults and, in the absence of contrary evidence, it is reasonable to extrapolate these to children over the age of five. This also applies to the guideline for non-starch polysaccharides, which has been derived from the DRV for adults to give a Calculated Reference Value for school meals.

How the nutritional guidelines for school meals have been compiled

The nutritional guidelines for school meals set out below are based on a review of the current nutritional status of school children, the estimated contribution of school meals to nutrient intake, and the government's most recent dietary guidelines. The Caroline Walker Trust Expert Working Group on Nutritional Guidelines for School Meals has considered the evidence in the light of their implications for health, and made recommendations accordingly.

Despite the lack of information regarding the functional importance of different intakes of many nutrients, the Working Group has accepted the DRVs as the best available quantified levels for the assessment of children's diets and for guidelines for school meals. The Reference Nutrient Intake (RNI) has been chosen as the appropriate DRV for planning food supplied in school meals. It will ensure that the needs of those with high nutrient requirements are catered for, and will be appropriate for most children, although some groups may have different requirements.

Nutrients which are recognised to be marginal in children's diets are recommended in an increased amount relative to the energy content of school meals. This is intended to protect individuals at risk of deficiency.

Using the nutritional guidelines

The guidelines provide figures for the recommended nutrient content of an average school meal provided for children over a one-week period.
They should be applied to the school meal food provided as a whole to the school population. They are intended to provide a basis for nutritional standards in the specifications for contracts set by LEAs and schools, and for menu planning and monitoring.

To achieve a good state of nutrition, the average intake of the group should meet the specified guidelines over a period of time. The length of that period varies from one nutrient to another, and from one individual to another. Furthermore, children's food intake varies from day to day. In the light of these facts, one week was considered as a pragmatic time period over which to base these nutritional guidelines for school meals, and the guidelines should be applied to the average meal provided rather than an individual plate of food consumed.

As the guidelines will be used for planning food supplied rather than that consumed, steps will need to be taken to optimise the nutritional quality of food in all stages of food preparation and service. Thus nutrient losses in cooking and storage will need to be minimised, and steps should be taken to promote healthier options and combinations of foods through careful marketing.

The quantitative guidelines will therefore need to be translated into qualitative guidelines and practical advice for caterers.

Lunchtime eating patterns among children in the UK have changed over the past decade. The cash cafeteria system and compulsory competitive tendering have had a major impact on school meals provision, and the school meals service has to compete with high street outlets. The marketing of foods and dishes by caterers will be important in determining children's choice of food, and whether they consume a healthy meal.

Table 5 and the text on pages 70-74 present a summary and rationale for the nutritional guidelines for school meals. Values for energy and quantities of nutrients for mixed schools are given in Tables 6 and 7. Appendix 1 gives details of DRVs and derived amounts by age and sex. Full tables of the nutritional guidelines for school meals can be found in Appendix 4, which gives quantities for energy and nutrients for different age, sex and school groups. A list of rich sources of nutrients is provided in Appendix 3.

While broad recommendations for the implementation of these nutritional guidelines are given in Chapter 7, it is beyond the scope of the report to give detailed practical advice on implementation.

Nutritional guidelines for school meals

The overall aim of these nutritional guidelines for school meals is to contribute to a diet which contains more bread, cereals and other starchy foods, more fruit and vegetables, and less fat, sugar and salty foods, and which is richer in minerals and vitamins.

The guidelines provide figures for the recommended nutrient content of an average school meal provided for children over a one-week period. In practical terms this is the total amount of food provided, divided by the number of children eating it, averaged over a week.

Table 5	SUMMARY OF NUTRITIONAL GUIDELINES FOR SCHOOL MEALS
ENERGY	30% of the Estimated Average Requirement (EAR)
FAT	Not more than 35% of food energy
SATURATED FATTY ACIDS	Not more than 11% of food energy
CARBOHYDRATE	Not less than 50% of food energy
NON-MILK EXTRINSIC SUGARS	Not more than 11% of food energy
NON-STARCH POLYSACCHARIDES ('fibre')	Not less than 30% of the Calculated Reference Value
PROTEIN	Not less than 30% of the Reference Nutrient Intake (RNI)
IRON	Not less than 40% of the Reference Nutrient Intake (RNI)
CALCIUM	Not less than 35% of the Reference Nutrient Intake (RNI)
VITAMIN A (retinol equivalents)	Not less than 30% of the Reference Nutrient Intake (RNI)
FOLATE	Not less than 40% of the Reference Nutrient Intake (RNI)
VITAMIN C	Not less than 35% of the Reference Nutrient Intake (RNI)
Sodium should be reduced in catering practice.	

ENERGY
30% of the Estimated Average Requirement (EAR)

The government's survey of school children's diets in 1983 found that, on average, children derive 30% of their energy from school meals. Although the average energy intake among school children is lower than the Estimated Average Requirement (EAR), children show no signs of under-nutrition. Indeed, overweight and obesity are now significant problems among adults and children in the UK. A balance between energy intake and energy expenditure through physical activity is important. Although eating patterns have changed, for many children, particularly those from low-income households, the school meal is the most important meal or the only substantial meal they will eat all day.

FAT
Not more than 35% of food energy

The COMA Panel recommended a reduction in total fat consumption to a population average of 35% of food energy. Studies have found that, on average, school children derive 37-40% of their energy from fat, and school meals may make a high contribution. The recommendations for fat are based on data from adults but, like previous COMA recommendations for fat, are applicable to children over the age of five. Apart from essential fatty acids, there is no absolute requirement for fats: the figure therefore represents a pragmatic maximum.

SATURATED FATTY ACIDS
Not more than 11% of food energy

The COMA Panel recommended a reduction in intake of saturated fatty acids to a population average of 11% of food energy, and no change in poly-unsaturated fatty acids. The individual fatty acids, myristic acid and palmitic acid, which are particularly likely to raise blood cholesterol levels, are found mainly in dairy products, meat, chocolate, cakes, hard margarine and soft margarines not made from polyunsaturated oils.

CARBOHYDRATE
Not less than 50% of food energy

Carbohydrate should provide the major food energy requirement for school children, and starches, together with intrinsic and milk sugars, should provide the main source of carbohydrate food energy, and an average of 39% of total food energy. The guideline for carbohydrate is the same as the Dietary

Reference Value. The DRVs are based on data from adults, and it is assumed here that the same principle can be applied to children. Complex carbohydrates are an important source of non-starch polysaccharides ('fibre') and of many vitamins and minerals. An increase in the starch component of the meals will compensate for the loss in energy resulting from a reduction in fats and non-milk extrinsic sugars.

NON-MILK EXTRINSIC SUGARS
Not more than 11% of food energy

For the first time, a national recommendation has been set for intake of sugar, representing a reduction in the current consumption by school children. The guideline for 'added' or non-milk extrinsic (NME) sugars – that is, sugars which are not part of the cellular structure of food, but excluding the sugar in milk or milk products – is as the DRV, a maximum of 11% of food energy, not exceeding about 60 grams per day. There is no absolute requirement for sugars. NME sugars include, for example, table sugar and sugar added to recipes, and are found in foods such as confectionery, cakes, biscuits, soft drinks and fruit juices. Concentrated sources of NME sugars should not be offered alone or outside meals.

NON-STARCH POLYSACCHARIDES ('fibre')
Not less than 30% of the Calculated Reference Value

A DRV for non-starch polysaccharides (NSP, or 'fibre') has been set for the first time. Cereals, pulses, vegetables and fruit are major sources of NSP. For adults, the DRV is 18 grams. The recommendation for children is that they should eat proportionately less NSP than adults, based on their smaller body size. The COMA Panel left open the determination of precisely how this should be translated for children. For pragmatic reasons, this has been calculated for these guidelines in proportion to the energy recommendations to give the Calculated Reference Value. The calculated NSP recommendation is 8 grams per 1,000 kcal.

PROTEIN
Not less than 30% of the Reference Nutrient Intake (RNI)

The RNIs for protein set by the COMA Panel on Dietary Reference Values represent the need for protein, and are based mainly on World Health Organization recommendations. They are slightly lower than the 1979 RDAs. Average protein intakes among children in the UK are above the RNI, and the recommendation is based on the contribution of school meals to the overall diet.

IRON
Not less than 40% of the Reference Nutrient Intake (RNI)

Surveys have indicated that many children have an iron intake which is lower than the RNI for iron. This is particularly true for adolescent girls. The source of iron is an important consideration, particularly for vegetarians and vegans, and up to a quarter of older girls are likely to be vegetarian. Hence a figure of 40% of the RNI has been set. The lunchtime meal is potentially an important source of iron, and school meals should make a major contribution to children's iron intake. In mixed schools, the highest iron guideline for the age group, ie the figure for girls, should be used to ensure that sufficient iron is available for girls.

CALCIUM
Not less than 35% of the Reference Nutrient Intake (RNI)

Surveys have indicated that the diets of children are relatively low in calcium. Milk contributed at least 30% of calcium to the diet of children in 1983, and the loss of free school milk may have had a serious impact on the calcium intake of some children. Although other meals, such as breakfast, can be important contributors of calcium, school meals should make a significant contribution to the calcium intake of school children. Hence a figure of 35% of the RNI has been set for school meals provision. In mixed schools, the highest calcium guideline for the age group, ie the figure for boys, should be used, to reflect the higher DRV for boys.

VITAMIN A (retinol equivalents)
Not less than 30% of the Reference Nutrient Intake (RNI)

There is evidence that the RNI for vitamin A is not being met in certain groups, such as children from low-income families and girls on low-energy diets. School meals could make an important contribution. However, there is evidence that a high retinol intake is a potential risk to the foetus in early pregnancy. Excessive retinol should therefore be avoided in secondary schools with girls. In practical terms, liver or liver products, which are rich sources of retinol, should not be provided more than once a week. Carotene, a precursor of vitamin A, found mainly in fruit and vegetables, has no known toxic effects.

FOLATE
Not less than 40% of the Reference Nutrient Intake (RNI)

Folate intakes among school children appear to be below the RNI. In addition to its role in the prevention of anaemia, there is good evidence that high intakes of folic acid can reduce the risk of recurrence of neural tube defects (NTD: spina bifida and anencephaly) in affected families. There is also suggestive, but not conclusive, evidence that folic acid/folate supplementation during the periconceptual period may reduce the risk of first occurrences of NTD. In view of this potential importance of folate in the prevention of these congenital deformities, it is appropriate to ensure as far as possible that intakes are adequate, particularly among girls who may be at risk of unplanned pregnancy. Hence a figure of 40% of the RNI has been set for school meals provision.

VITAMIN C
Not less than 35% of the Reference Nutrient Intake (RNI)

Although surveys show that most children have adequate vitamin C intakes, there is a strong social class and regional gradient, with lower intakes among children in the north of England and Scotland, and in lower socioeconomic groups. School meals can make a significant contribution to vitamin C intake. However, there may be a problem in providing adequate vitamin C while also meeting the other nutritional guidelines, and care therefore needs to be taken to preserve the vitamin C content of school meals. A guideline of 35% has therefore been set. Vitamin C will also assist the absorption of the suggested increased iron content in the meal. Rich sources of vitamin C are given in Appendix 3, although care needs to be taken in cooking methods, to preserve this heat sensitive vitamin.

Sodium should be reduced in catering practice.

The government's Panel on Dietary Reference Values pointed out that the physiological requirements for sodium are low, and current sodium intakes are needlessly high. The Panel accepted the possibility that there may be public health benefits from a reduced sodium intake. Hence the nutritional guideline for school meals is that sodium should be reduced in catering practice.

These nutritional guidelines cover identified nutritional problems that can feasibly and appropriately be addressed in school meals provision.

They are not intended to cover all nutritional issues. For example, vegetarians and vegans have a potential risk of low vitamin B12 intakes. This is of concern among school children because up to a quarter of teenage girls now claim to be vegetarian or vegan. At present, however, there is no clinical evidence of a deficiency among this group.

Also, vitamin D deficiency may be a potential problem for children who are not exposed to sufficient sunshine. This applies particularly to children who do not have the opportunity to go outside during the day, such as those at schools with no playground; children who are covered up by clothing for cultural reasons; and children living in northern areas of the UK. If physical education involving outdoor activities is a normal part of the school curriculum, it is likely that pupils will have adequate tissue levels of vitamin D. Rich sources of vitamin D are given in Appendix 3.

School meals alone cannot achieve ideal eating patterns among school children: there are other potential nutritional problems which may be more appropriately addressed outside school meals provision. School meals can, however, make a valuable and significant contribution to the nutrition and health of children, and these nutritional guidelines for school meals should help achieve that goal.

REFERENCES

1   National Advisory Committee on Nutrition Education (NACNE). 1983. *Proposals for nutritional guidelines for health education in Britain*. London: Health Education Council.

2   Department of Health and Social Security. 1984. *Diet and cardiovascular disease. Committee on Medical Aspects of Food Policy: report of the Panel on Diet in Relation to Cardiovascular Disease*. Report on health and social subjects 28. London: HMSO.

3   The Coronary Prevention Group and British Dietetic Association. 1987. *Diet or disease? The case for school meals guidelines*. London: The Coronary Prevention Group.

4   Department of Health and Social Security. 1979. *Recommended Daily Amounts of food energy and nutrients for groups of people in the United Kingdom*. Report on health and social subjects 15. London: HMSO.

5   Department of Health. 1991. *Dietary Reference Values for food energy and nutrients for the United Kingdom. Report of the Panel on Dietary Reference Values of the Committee on Medical Aspects of Food Policy*. Report on health and social subjects 41. London: HMSO.

Table 6	Nutritional guidelines for school meals INFANT, JUNIOR AND SECONDARY SCHOOLS: ALL PUPILS

These guidelines provide figures for the recommended nutrient content of an average school meal provided for children over a one-week period. In practical terms this is the total amount of food provided, divided by the number of children eating it, averaged over a week. Fuller tables for single sex schools are given in Appendix 4.

	ENERGY	FAT	SAT FATTY ACIDS	CARBO-HYDRATE	NME SUGARS	NSP	PROTEIN	IRON	CALCIUM	VITAMIN A (retinol equivalents)	FOLATE	VITAMIN C
	30% of EAR	Not more than 35% of food energy*	Not more than 11% of food energy*	Not less than 50% of food energy	Not more than 11% of food energy*	Not less than 30% of Calculated Reference Value**	Not less than 30% of RNI	Not less than 40% of RNI	Not less than 35% of RNI	Not less than 30% of RNI	Not less than 40% of RNI	Not less than 35% of RNI
	MJ/kcal	MAX* g	MAX* g	MIN g	MAX* g	MIN g	MIN g	MIN mg	MIN mg	MIN µg	MIN µg	MIN mg
INFANTS 5-6 years***	2.04MJ 489kcal	19.0	6.0	65.2	14.3	3.9	5.9	2.4	158	150	40	11
JUNIOR 7-10 years	2.33MJ 557kcal	21.7	6.8	74.3	16.3	4.5	8.5	3.5	193	150	60	11
SECONDARY Not including 6th form 11-16 years	2.65MJ 634kcal	24.7	7.7	84.5	18.0	5.1	13.0	5.9	350	183	80	13
SIXTH FORM ONLY 17-18 years***	3.05MJ 730kcal	28.4	8.9	97.3	18.0	5.9	15.0	5.9	350	195	80	14
ALL SECONDARY Including 6th form 11-18 years	2.70MJ 646kcal	25.1	7.9	86.1	18.0	5.2	13.3	5.9	350	185	80	13

Abbreviations
DRV   Dietary Reference Value
EAR   Estimated Average Requirement
NME SUGARS   Non-milk extrinsic sugars
NSP   Non-starch polysaccharides
RNI   Reference Nutrient Intake
SAT FATTY ACIDS Saturated fatty acids

SODIUM should be reduced in catering practice.

*   As there is no absolute requirement for sugars or fats (except essential fatty acids), these values represent a maximum.

** The Dietary Reference Value for non-starch polysaccharides is 18g for adults, and children should eat proportionately less, based on their lower body size. For pragmatic reasons, this has been calculated for these guidelines as a percentage of the energy recommendation, to give the Calculated Reference Value. The calculated NSP guideline is 8g per 1,000 kcal.

*** For infants and sixth forms, the values presented here may be slightly too low, particularly for energy. However, this is only of the order of 3–5% below what the value should be. This is due to the fact that the DRVs are presented for wider age bands including younger children, namely 4–6 year olds and 15–18 year olds.

THE CAROLINE WALKER TRUST, 1992

Table 7

Nutritional guidelines for school meals
FIRST, MIDDLE AND UPPER SCHOOLS: ALL PUPILS

These guidelines provide figures for the recommended nutrient content of an average school meal provided for children over a one-week period. In practical terms this is the total amount of food provided, divided by the number of children eating it, averaged over a week. Fuller tables for single sex schools are given in Appendix 4.

	ENERGY	FAT	SAT FATTY ACIDS	CARBO-HYDRATE	NME SUGARS	NSP	PROTEIN	IRON	CALCIUM	VITAMIN A (retinol equivalents)	FOLATE	VITAMIN C
	30% of EAR	Not more than 35% of food energy*	Not more than 11% of food energy*	Not less than 50% of food energy	Not more than 11% of food energy*	Not less than 30% of Calculated Reference Value**	Not less than 30% of RNI	Not less than 40% of RNI	Not less than 35% of RNI	Not less than 30% of RNI	Not less than 40% of RNI	Not less than 35% of RNI
	MJ/kcal	MAX* g	MAX* g	MIN g	MAX* g	MIN g	MIN g	MIN mg	MIN mg	MIN μg	MIN μg	MIN mg
FIRST 5-8 years	2.19MJ 523kcal	20.3	6.4	69.7	15.3	4.2	7.2	3.0	175	150	50	11
MIDDLE 9-13 years	2.46MJ 589kcal	22.9	7.2	78.5	17.3	4.7	10.9	4.9	287	168	72	12
UPPER 14-18 years	2.85MJ 682kcal	26.5	8.3	90.9	18.0	5.5	14.1	5.9	350	189	80	13

SODIUM should be reduced in catering practice.

* As there is no absolute requirement for sugars or fats (except essential fatty acids), these values represent a maximum.

** The Dietary Reference Value for non-starch polysaccharides is 18g for adults, and children should eat proportionately less, based on their lower body size. For pragmatic reasons, this has been calculated for these guidelines as a percentage of the energy recommendation, to give the Calculated Reference Value. The calculated NSP guideline is 8g per 1,000 kcal.

Abbreviations
DRV   Dietary Reference Value
EAR   Estimated Average Requirement
NME SUGARS   Non-milk extrinsic sugars
NSP   Non-starch polysaccharides
RNI   Reference Nutrient Intake
SAT FATTY ACIDS   Saturated fatty acids

CHAPTER 7

Implementing the nutritional guidelines

School meals provide a vital social service for some children. They also present a major opportunity to achieve healthy eating habits and an awareness of diet and health for all children, particularly when they are supported by nutrition education in the classroom. But in order to be successful, school meals need to be a positive and enjoyable experience, since the service often has to compete with high street shops and cafes for its customers.

This report sets nutritional guidelines for the average school meal on offer, but marketing is important to encourage the uptake of school meals and of the healthier options. With the widespread cash cafeteria system, children have more choice and will respond to incentives to choose healthy meals, which should be available throughout the entire service.

This chapter gives broad recommendations for implementing the nutritional guidelines, including recommendations in the areas of: policy; purchasing and providing; marketing and education; and monitoring. It thus covers both the *provision of foods* and the *environmental influences* which affect choice. However, a long-term commitment to a healthy school meals service is crucial, at both national and local levels.

There is also a need for extensive menu and recipe development, to translate the quantified nutritional guidelines into practical advice for caterers. A later report, in collaboration with caterers, is planned to give more specific guidance on turning the nutritional guidelines into healthy meal provision, with examples of good practice.

Policy

School meals can be an important aspect of the health promoting school – the school in which the healthy choices are the easy choices. The role of school meals in providing nutrition education to children needs to be fully recognised by caterers, teachers, head teachers, governors and parents.

The 'healthy schools' initiative outlined in the government's White Paper, *The health of the nation*, provides an opportunity to help ensure that the provision of food in schools reflects classroom teaching about food and health.

1   **Every school should adopt and implement a school nutrition policy which covers both the teaching of nutrition and the provision of food within the school environment.**
     The policy should include school meals, tuck shops, vending machines, food vans and promotional activities, as well as classroom teaching. The nutritional implications of all school initiatives should be considered as part of this policy.

2   **In-service training of school meals caterers and of those serving and supervising the meals is essential if these guidelines are to be achieved.**
     Training programmes will need to include basic nutritional knowledge, practical preparation methods, the links between food and health, and marketing techniques to encourage the choice of healthy meals. The influential role of those serving school meals could be developed.

3   **Schools should provide a range of meals which meet the nutritional guidelines and which take account of health, religious and ethnic preferences.**
     For example, school meals should always include a variety of interesting vegetarian options.

4   **In order to help achieve these guidelines for school meals, the government should work towards a renegotiation of the EC subsidy for milks, cheese and yoghurts served in schools.**
     The aim should be to achieve a subsidy for low-fat varieties that is the same, or higher than, that for full-fat varieties.

Purchasing and providing

Support from the purchasers and the providers of school meals for the implementation of the nutritional guidelines, and liaison between the two groups, is crucial to the success of these guidelines. A multi-disciplinary working group may facilitate the early stages of implementation.

5   **Local education authorities (LEAs) and schools should draw up nutritional specifications for school meals tenders in line with the nutritional guidelines in this report.**
     Local community dietitians are important in providing advice and support in the development of such nutritional specifications. The specifications will need to be realistic and achievable, and the means of monitoring them should be clearly identified in contracts.

6   **Caterers and/or LEA purchasing consortia could cooperate to develop nutritional specifications for all major commodities and foods used in schools.**

7 **The nutritional guidelines contained in this report should be implemented gradually.**
This could be done, for example, through changes in menu planning and recipes, and substitution of ingredients. Long-term strategies are needed, with step-by-step implementation and agreed objectives, over and above any short-term promotions.

8 **The cost of school meals needs to be addressed by both purchasers and providers, at various levels.**
Cost is a primary consideration, and the uptake of meals will always depend to some extent on price, as well as quality. Consideration should be given to subsidies as well as meal-pricing policies.

Marketing and education

If children are to be attracted to eat school meals, then the challenge to caterers is to provide a service which competes with high street outlets in terms of promotion and presentation as well as price, content and availability. This is particularly important in secondary schools. Budgetary considerations are paramount in school meals catering, although there are indications that healthier meals can be achieved within a realistic budget.

9 **Attention needs to be given to the marketing and presentation of the food to make it attractive to children.**
This might include the names of dishes and the way the food is presented, both on the counter, and on the plate. The surroundings in which school meals are eaten are important to their appeal. Lunchtime eating areas should be comfortable and attractive to children, and well supervised.

10 **Caterers should consider pricing policies which encourage the take-up of healthier options**.
Healthier options could be sold at lower prices. Healthy eating can also be encouraged by selective control of portion sizes. In cash cafeterias, foods might be 'tied' to provide a nutritional balance in the foods served together, for example by giving a 'free' portion of vegetables with each portion of chips.

11 **Advertising the school meals service to parents and children is an important part of any marketing strategy.**
Parental interest and involvement can be extended through menu leaflets and through tasting sessions on open days or parent evenings.

12 **Education about food and health in the classroom is important to the implementation of these guidelines.**
Children should be equipped with the knowledge and skills to eat well

on the basis of broad nutrition principles. In the National Curriculum, Science, Technology, and Curriculum Guidance 5 on health education all make provision for teaching on food and nutrition, and the contribution of school meals could be included in this.

13 **There needs to be systematic liaison between those involved in classroom education and those providing school meals, to help ensure that food provision in the school is consistent with and reinforces classroom messages about healthy eating.**
The canteen can be used as a learning environment. Teachers and health professionals should work with caterers to promote and provide information on selecting healthy school meals – including their nutritional content – to pupils, staff, parents and governors.

Monitoring

Monitoring of the implementation of the nutritional guidelines is crucial for successful implementation, to ensure that the nutritional guidelines are being met, and to provide feedback to the purchasers, providers and consumers of school meals.

14 **Regular monitoring of school meals provision should be included in contracts and be undertaken by the LEA or school.**
This should include monitoring of nutritional specifications in tendering, menu planning and meal provision, and uptake of meals.

15 **Governing bodies and school boards should require an annual report on the provision and uptake of school meals, and foods from tuck shops, vans and vending machines within their school, with particular regard to nutrition.**
Governing bodies should consider nominating an individual governor with responsibility for monitoring the implementation of the school nutrition policy.

APPENDIX I

Dietary Reference Values and derived amounts for children aged 4-18

Table 8   DIETARY REFERENCE VALUES AND DERIVED AMOUNTS FOR NUTRIENTS PER DAY: BOYS

These guidelines are intended to provide an average daily intake over a period of time, such as a week.

	ENERGY	FAT	SAT FATTY ACIDS	CARBO-HYDRATE	NME SUGARS	NSP	PROTEIN	IRON	CALCIUM	VITAMIN A (retinol equivalents)	FOLATE	VITAMIN C
Dietary Reference Value (DRV)	EAR	DRV: average 35% of food energy*	DRV: average 11% of food energy*	DRV: average 50% of food energy	DRV: average 11% of food energy (max 60g)*	Proportion of DRV for adults (18g)/CRV**	RNI	RNI	RNI	RNI	RNI	RNI
	MJ/kcal	g	g	g	g	g	g	mg	mg	μg	μg	mg
4-6 YEARS	7.16MJ 1,715kcal	66.7	21.0	228.7	50.3	13.7	19.7	6.1	450	500	100	30
7-10 YEARS	8.24MJ 1,970kcal	76.6	24.1	262.7	57.8	15.8	28.3	8.7	550	500	150	30
11-14 YEARS	9.27MJ 2,220kcal	86.3	27.1	296.0	60.0	17.8	42.1	11.3	1,000	600	200	35
15-18 YEARS	11.51MJ 2,755kcal	107.1	33.7	367.3	60.0	22.1	55.2	11.3	1,000	700	200	40

*   As there is no absolute requirement for sugars or fats (except essential fatty acids), these values represent a maximum.

** The Dietary Reference Value for non-starch polysaccharides is 18g for adults, and children should eat proportionately less, based on their lower body size. For pragmatic reasons, this has been calculated for these guidelines as a percentage of the energy recommendation, to give the Calculated Reference Value. The calculated NSP guideline is 8g per 1,000 kcal.

Abbreviations
DRV   Dietary Reference Value
EAR   Estimated Average Requirement
NME SUGARS   Non-milk extrinsic sugars
NSP   Non-starch polysaccharides
RNI   Reference Nutrient Intake
SAT FATTY ACIDS   Saturated fatty acids

Table 9 DIETARY REFERENCE VALUES AND DERIVED AMOUNTS FOR NUTRIENTS PER DAY: *GIRLS*

These guidelines are intended to provide an average daily intake over a period of time, such as a week.

Dietary Reference Value (DRV)	ENERGY EAR	FAT DRV: average 35% of food energy*	SAT FATTY ACIDS DRV: average 11% of food energy*	CARBO-HYDRATE DRV: average 50% of food energy	NME SUGARS DRV: average 11% of food energy (max 60g)*	NSP Proportion of DRV for adults (18g)/CRV**	PROTEIN RNI	IRON RNI	CALCIUM RNI	VITAMIN A (retinol equivalents) RNI	FOLATE RNI	VITAMIN C RNI
	MJ/kcal	g	g	g	g	g	g	mg	mg	µg	µg	mg
4–6 YEARS	6.46MJ 1,545kcal	60.1	18.9	206.0	45.3	12.4	19.7	6.1	450	500	100	30
7–10 YEARS	7.28MJ 1,740kcal	67.7	21.3	232.0	51.0	14.0	28.3	8.7	550	500	150	30
11–14 YEARS	7.72MJ 1,845kcal	71.8	22.6	246.0	54.1	14.8	41.2	14.8	800	600	200	35
15–18 YEARS	8.83MJ 2,110kcal	82.1	25.8	281.3	60.0	16.9	45.0	14.8	800	600	200	40

* As there is no absolute requirement for sugars or fats (except essential fatty acids), these values represent a maximum.

** The Dietary Reference Value for non-starch polysaccharides is 18g for adults, and children should eat proportionately less, based on their lower body size. For pragmatic reasons, this has been calculated for these guidelines as a percentage of the energy recommendation, to give the Calculated Reference Value. The calculated NSP guideline is 8g per 1,000 kcal.

Abbreviations
DRV   Dietary Reference Value
EAR   Estimated Average Requirement
NME SUGARS   Non-milk extrinsic sugars
NSP   Non-starch polysaccharides
RNI   Reference Nutrient Intake
SAT FATTY ACIDS   Saturated fatty acids

APPENDIX 2

Previous nutritional guidelines for school meals

Table 10	PREVIOUS NUTRITIONAL GUIDELINES FOR SCHOOL MEALS	

	Proposed Education (Nutritional Requirements) Bill, 1987[1]	**Diet or disease: the case for school meals guidelines**[2] (The Coronary Prevention Group/ British Dietetic Association, 1987)
ENERGY	Minimum requirement 30% of RDA	Not less than 30% of RDA
FAT	Maximum requirement 35% of energy	33–35% of energy ie approximately 32g per meal
CARBOHYDRATE	Minimum requirement 54% energy provided	54% of total energy
ADDED SUGARS	Maximum 10% of total energy	No more than 10% of total energy ie no more than 25g per meal
FIBRE	Minimum requirement 12g per 1,000 kcal	30% of daily intake or approximately 8g
PROTEIN	Minimum requirement 11% energy provided	11% of total energy
IRON	Minimum content 45% of RDA	Not less than 35–40% of RDA
CALCIUM	Minimum content 30% of RDA	No recommendations made
VITAMIN A (retinol equivalents)	Minimum content 30% of RDA	Not less than 35% of RDA
VITAMIN C	Minimum content 50% of RDA	Not less than 50% of RDA

REFERENCES

1 Proposed *Education (Nutritional Requirements) Bill, 1987. A Bill to amend the 1980 Education Act to make provision with respect to nutritional requirements for school meals and for connected purposes.*
2 The Coronary Prevention Group and British Dietetic Association. 1987. *Diet or disease? The case for school meals guidelines.* London: The Coronary Prevention Group.

APPENDIX 3

Rich sources of nutrients

| Table II | | **RICH SOURCES OF NUTRIENTS** | | | |

The nutritional guidelines outlined in this report highlight the importance of an adequate supply of certain essential minerals and vitamins. This Table lists a number of foods which are rich in or are important sources of these nutrients. The figures are based on average *adult* servings. Children's servings will be proportional to adult servings, depending on age. Foods are arranged in descending order of value.

	IRON	CALCIUM	VITAMIN A	FOLATE	VITAMIN C	VITAMIN D
HIGH	over 5mg	over 300mg	over 500µg	over 100µg	over 40mg	over 1µg
	pig liver kidney chicken liver All Bran liver sausage/ pate	tofu spinach sardines cheese	pig liver chicken liver liver sausage/ pate carrots spinach cantaloupe melon sweet potatoes dried apricots fresh/canned apricots	chicken liver spinach	blackcurrants canned guava orange grapefruit melon	herrings pilchards sardines tuna canned salmon egg
INTERMEDIATE	2-5mg	150–300mg	100-500µg	40-100µg	20-40mg	0.5-1µg
	beef lamb spinach Weetabix sardines corned beef pilchards soya beans beefburger curry powder chick peas dried apricots lentils wholemeal bread/ flour	pilchards yoghurt milk (whole/ skimmed)	nectarine watercress tomatoes peach cabbage (dark) margarine kidney brussel sprouts runner beans cheese broad beans butter blackcurrants	yeast extract kidney pig liver brussel sprouts orange melon All Bran peas cabbage cauliflower	canned gooseberries brussel sprouts canned grapefruit green pepper broccoli cabbage cauliflower spinach	pig liver liver sausage/pate

Table 11 (cont)

MODERATE	1-2mg	50-150mg	40-100µg	20-40µg	10-20mg	0.2-0.5µg
	baked beans	canned salmon	peas	broccoli	satsumas	chicken liver
	muesli	evaporated milk	canned salmon	wholemeal	potatoes	
	sausage	muesli	honeydew melon	bread/flour	eating apples	
	black-eyed peas	white bread/flour	egg	runner beans	nectarines	
	blackcurrants	orange	herrings	tomatoes		
	salmon		sweetcorn	beef		
	white bread		prunes	ackee		
	chicken		orange	white bread/flour		
	herrings			Weetabix		
	egg			peanuts		
	broad beans			parsnip		
	tofu			potatoes		
	black treacle					

Note
Excessive retinol should be avoided in secondary schools with girls.
In practical terms, liver or liver products should not be provided more
than once a week

APPENDIX 4

Nutritional guidelines for school meals: TABLES

The overall aim of these nutritional guidelines for school meals is to contribute to a diet which contains more bread, cereals and other starchy foods, more fruit and vegetables, and less fat, sugar and salty foods, and which is richer in minerals and vitamins.

The guidelines provide figures for the recommended nutrient content of an average school meal provided for children over a one-week period. In practical terms this is the total amount of food provided, divided by the number of children eating it, averaged over a week.

Table 12	SUMMARY OF NUTRITIONAL GUIDELINES FOR SCHOOL MEALS
ENERGY	30% of the Estimated Average Requirement (EAR)
FAT	Not more than 35% of food energy
SATURATED FATTY ACIDS	Not more than 11% of food energy
CARBOHYDRATE	Not less than 50% of food energy
NON-MILK EXTRINSIC SUGARS	Not more than 11% of food energy
NON-STARCH POLYSACCHARIDES ('fibre')	Not less than 30% of the Calculated Reference Value
PROTEIN	Not less than 30% of the Reference Nutrient Intake (RNI)
IRON	Not less than 40% of the Reference Nutrient Intake (RNI)
CALCIUM	Not less than 35% of the Reference Nutrient Intake (RNI)
VITAMIN A (retinol equivalents)	Not less than 30% of the Reference Nutrient Intake (RNI)
FOLATE	Not less than 40% of the Reference Nutrient Intake (RNI)
VITAMIN C	Not less than 35% of the Reference Nutrient Intake (RNI)
Sodium should be reduced in catering practice.	

Table 13 Nutritional guidelines for school meals: BOYS

These guidelines provide figures for the recommended nutrient content of an average school meal provided for children over a one-week period. In practical terms this is the total amount of food provided, divided by the number of children eating it, averaged over a week.

	ENERGY	FAT	SAT FATTY ACIDS	CARBO-HYDRATE	NME SUGARS	NSP	PROTEIN	IRON	CALCIUM	VITAMIN A (retinol equivalents)	FOLATE	VITAMIN C
	30% of EAR	Not more than 35% of food energy*	Not more than 11% of food energy*	Not less than 50% of food energy	Not more than 11% of food energy*	Not less than 30% of Calculated Reference Value**	Not less than 30% of RNI	Not less than 40% of RNI	Not less than 35% of RNI	Not less than 30% of RNI	Not less than 40% of RNI	Not less than 35% of RNI
	MJ/kcal	MAX* g	MAX* g	MIN g	MAX* g	MIN g	MIN g	MIN mg	MIN mg	MIN µg	MIN µg	MIN mg
4-6 YEARS	2.15MJ 515kcal	20.0	6.3	68.7	15.1	4.1	5.9	2.4	158	150	40	11
7-10 YEARS	2.47MJ 591kcal	23.0	7.2	78.8	17.3	4.7	8.5	3.5	193	150	60	11
11-14 YEARS	2.78MJ 666kcal	25.9	8.1	88.8	18.0	5.3	12.6	4.5	350	180	80	12
15-18 YEARS	3.45MJ 827kcal	32.2	10.1	110.3	18.0	6.6	16.6	4.5	350	210	80	14

SODIUM should be reduced in catering practice.

* As there is no absolute requirement for sugars or fats (except essential fatty acids), these values represent a maximum.

** The Dietary Reference Value for non-starch polysaccharides is 18g for adults, and children should eat proportionately less, based on their lower body size. For pragmatic reasons, this has been calculated for these guidelines as a percentage of the energy recommendation, to give the Calculated Reference Value. The calculated NSP guideline is 8g per 1,000 kcal.

Abbreviations
DRV   Dietary Reference Value
EAR   Estimated Average Requirement
NME SUGARS   Non-milk extrinsic sugars
NSP   Non-starch polysaccharides
RNI   Reference Nutrient Intake
SAT FATTY ACIDS   Saturated fatty acids

Table 14   Nutritional guidelines for school meals: GIRLS

These guidelines provide figures for the recommended nutrient content of an average school meal provided for children over a one-week period. In practical terms this is the total amount of food provided, divided by the number of children eating it, averaged over a week.

	ENERGY	FAT	SAT FATTY ACIDS	CARBO- HYDRATE	NME SUGARS	NSP	PROTEIN	IRON	CALCIUM	VITAMIN A (retinol equivalents)	FOLATE	VITAMIN C
	30% of EAR	Not more than 35% of food energy*	Not more than 11% of food energy*	Not less than 50% of food energy	Not more than 11% of food energy*	Not less than 30% of Calculated Reference Value**	Not less than 30% of RNI	Not less than 40% of RNI	Not less than 35% of RNI	Not less than 30% of RNI	Not less than 40% of RNI	Not less than 35% of RNI
	MJ/kcal	MAX* g	MAX* g	MIN g	MAX* g	MIN g	MIN g	MIN mg	MIN mg	MIN µg	MIN µg	MIN mg
4-6 YEARS	1.94MJ 464kcal	18.0	5.7	61.9	13.6	3.7	5.9	2.4	158	150	40	11
7-10 YEARS	2.18MJ 522kcal	20.3	6.4	69.6	15.3	4.2	8.5	3.5	193	150	60	11
11-14 YEARS	2.32MJ 554kcal	21.5	6.8	73.9	16.3	4.4	12.4	5.9	280	180	80	12
15-18 YEARS	2.65MJ 633kcal	24.6	7.7	84.4	18.0	5.1	13.5	5.9	280	180	80	14

SODIUM should be reduced in catering practice.

*   As there is no absolute requirement for sugars or fats (except essential fatty acids), these values represent a maximum.

**   The Dietary Reference Value for non-starch polysaccharides is 18g for adults, and children should eat proportionately less, based on their lower body size. For pragmatic reasons, this has been calculated for these guidelines as a percentage of the energy recommendation, to give the Calculated Reference Value. The calculated NSP guideline is 8g per 1,000 kcal.

Abbreviations
DRV   Dietary Reference Value
EAR   Estimated Average Requirement
NME SUGARS   Non-milk extrinsic sugars
NSP   Non-starch polysaccharides
RNI   Reference Nutrient Intake
SAT FATTY ACIDS   Saturated fatty acids

THE CAROLINE WALKER TRUST, 1992

Table 15 — Nutritional guidelines for school meals
INFANT, JUNIOR AND SECONDARY SCHOOLS: ALL PUPILS

These guidelines provide figures for the recommended nutrient content of an average school meal provided for children over a one-week period. In practical terms this is the total amount of food provided, divided by the number of children eating it, averaged over a week.

	ENERGY	FAT	SAT FATTY ACIDS	CARBO-HYDRATE	NME SUGARS	NSP	PROTEIN	IRON	CALCIUM	VITAMIN A (retinol equivalents)	FOLATE	VITAMIN C
	30% of EAR	Not more than 35% of food energy*	Not more than 11% of food energy*	Not less than 50% of food energy	Not more than 11% of food energy*	Not less than 30% of Calculated Reference Value**	Not less than 30% of RNI	Not less than 40% of RNI	Not less than 35% of RNI	Not less than 30% of RNI	Not less than 40% of RNI	Not less than 35% of RNI
		MAX*	MAX*	MIN	MAX*	MIN	MIN	MIN	MIN	MIN	MIN	MIN
	MJ/kcal	g	g	g	g	g	g	mg	mg	µg	µg	mg
INFANTS 5–6 years***	2.04MJ 489kcal	19.0	6.0	65.2	14.3	3.9	5.9	2.4	158	150	40	11
JUNIOR 7–10 years	2.33MJ 557kcal	21.7	6.8	74.3	16.3	4.5	8.5	3.5	193	150	60	11
SECONDARY Not including 6th form 11–16 years	2.65MJ 634kcal	24.7	7.7	84.5	18.0	5.1	13.0	5.9	350	183	80	13
SIXTH FORM ONLY 17–18 years***	3.05MJ 730kcal	28.4	8.9	97.3	18.0	5.9	15.0	5.9	350	195	80	14
ALL SECONDARY Including 6th form 11–18 years	2.70MJ 646kcal	25.1	7.9	86.1	18.0	5.2	13.3	5.9	350	185	80	13

SODIUM should be reduced in catering practice.

* As there is no absolute requirement for sugars or fats (except essential fatty acids), these values represent a maximum.

** The Dietary Reference Value for non-starch polysaccharides is 18g for adults, and children should eat proportionately less, based on their lower body size. For pragmatic reasons, this has been calculated for these guidelines as a percentage of the energy recommendation, to give the Calculated Reference Value. The calculated NSP guideline is 8g per 1,000 kcal.

*** For infants and sixth forms, the values presented here may be slightly too low, particularly for energy. However, this is only of the order of 3–5% below what the value should be. This is due to the fact that the DRVs are presented for wider age bands including younger children, namely 4–6 year olds and 15–18 year olds.

Abbreviations
DRV — Dietary Reference Value
EAR — Estimated Average Requirement
NME SUGARS — Non-milk extrinsic sugars
NSP — Non-starch polysaccharides
RNI — Reference Nutrient Intake
SAT FATTY ACIDS — Saturated fatty acids

Table 16 — Nutritional guidelines for school meals
INFANT, JUNIOR AND SECONDARY SCHOOLS: BOYS

These guidelines provide figures for the recommended nutrient content of an average school meal provided for children over a one-week period. In practical terms this is the total amount of food provided, divided by the number of children eating it, averaged over a week.

	ENERGY	FAT	SAT FATTY ACIDS	CARBO-HYDRATE	NME SUGARS	NSP	PROTEIN	IRON	CALCIUM	VITAMIN A (retinol equivalents)	FOLATE	VITAMIN C
	30% of EAR	Not more than 35% of food energy*	Not more than 11% of food energy*	Not less than 50% of food energy	Not more than 11% of food energy*	Not less than 30% of Calculated Reference Value**	Not less than 30% of RNI	Not less than 40% of RNI	Not less than 35% of RNI	Not less than 30% of RNI	Not less than 40% of RNI	Not less than 35% of RNI
	MJ/kcal	MAX* g	MAX* g	MIN g	MAX* g	MIN g	MIN g	MIN mg	MIN mg	MIN µg	MIN µg	MIN mg
INFANTS 5-6 years***	2.15MJ 515kcal	20.0	6.3	68.7	15.1	4.1	5.9	2.4	158	150	40	11
JUNIOR 7-10 years	2.47MJ 591kcal	23.0	7.2	78.8	17.3	4.7	8.5	3.5	193	150	60	11
SECONDARY Not including 6th form 11-16 years	2.92MJ 698kcal	27.1	8.5	93.1	18.0	5.6	13.4	4.5	350	186	80	13
SECONDARY 6th form only*** 17-18 years	3.45MJ 827kcal	32.2	10.1	110.3	18.0	6.6	16.6	4.5	350	210	80	14
ALL SECONDARY Including 6th form 11-18 years	2.98MJ 714kcal	27.8	8.7	95.2	18.0	5.7	13.8	4.5	350	189	80	13

SODIUM should be reduced in catering practice.

* As there is no absolute requirement for sugars or fats (except essential fatty acids), these values represent a maximum.
** The Dietary Reference Value for non–starch polysaccharides is 18g for adults, and children should eat proportionately less, based on their lower body size. For pragmatic reasons, this has been calculated for these guidelines as a percentage of the energy recommendation, to give the Calculated Reference Value. The calculated NSP guideline is 8g per 1,000 kcal.
*** For infants and sixth forms, the values presented here may be slightly too low, particularly for energy. However, this is only of the order of 3–5% below what the value should be. This is due to the fact that the DRVs are presented for wider age bands including younger children, namely 4–6 year olds and 15–18 year olds.

Abbreviations
DRV — Dietary Reference Value
EAR — Estimated Average Requirement
NME SUGARS — Non-milk extrinsic sugars
NSP — Non-starch polysaccharides
RNI — Reference Nutrient Intake
SAT FATTY ACIDS — Saturated fatty acids

THE CAROLINE WALKER TRUST. 1992

Table 17 Nutritional guidelines for school meals
INFANT, JUNIOR AND SECONDARY SCHOOLS: *GIRLS*

These guidelines provide figures for the recommended nutrient content of an average school meal provided for children over a one-week period. In practical terms this is the total amount of food provided, divided by the number of children eating it, averaged over a week.

	ENERGY	FAT	SAT FATTY ACIDS	CARBO-HYDRATE	NME SUGARS	NSP	PROTEIN	IRON	CALCIUM	VITAMIN A (retinol equivalents)	FOLATE	VITAMIN C
	30% of EAR	Not more than 35% of food energy*	Not more than 11% of food energy*	Not less than 50% of food energy	Not more than 11% of food energy*	Not less than 30% of Calculated Reference Value**	Not less than 30% of RNI	Not less than 40% of RNI	Not less than 35% of RNI	Not less than 30% of RNI	Not less than 40% of RNI	Not less than 35% of RNI
	MJ/kcal	MAX* g	MAX* g	MIN g	MAX* g	MIN g	MIN g	MIN mg	MIN mg	MIN µg	MIN µg	MIN mg
INFANTS 5-6 years***	1.94MJ 464kcal	18.0	5.7	61.9	13.6	3.7	5.9	2.4	158	150	40	11
JUNIOR 7-10 years	2.18MJ 522kcal	20.3	6.4	69.6	15.3	4.2	8.5	3.5	193	150	60	11
SECONDARY Not including 6th form 11-16 years	2.38MJ 569kcal	22.1	7.0	75.9	16.7	4.6	12.6	5.9	280	180	80	13
SECONDARY 6th form only*** 17-18 years	2.65MJ 633kcal	24.6	7.7	84.4	18.0	5.1	13.5	5.9	280	180	80	14
ALL SECONDARY Including 6th form 11-18 years	2.41MJ 577kcal	22.4	7.1	76.9	16.9	4.6	12.7	5.9	280	180	80	13

SODIUM should be reduced in catering practice.

* As there is no absolute requirement for sugars or fats (except essential fatty acids), these values represent a maximum.
** The Dietary Reference Value for non–starch polysaccharides is 18g for adults, and children should eat proportionately less, based on their lower body size. For pragmatic reasons, this has been calculated for these guidelines as a percentage of the energy recommendation, to give the Calculated Reference Value. The calculated NSP guideline is 8g per 1,000 kcal.
*** For infants and sixth forms, the values presented here may be slightly too low, particularly for energy. However, this is only of the order of 3–5% below what the value should be. This is due to the fact that the DRVs are presented for wider age bands including younger children, namely 4–6 year olds and 15–18 year olds.

Abbreviations
DRV — Dietary Reference Value
EAR — Estimated Average Requirement
NME SUGARS — Non-milk extrinsic sugars
NSP — Non–starch polysaccharides
RNI — Reference Nutrient Intake
SAT FATTY ACIDS — Saturated fatty acids

Table 18 — Nutritional guidelines for school meals
FIRST, MIDDLE AND UPPER SCHOOLS: ALL PUPILS

These guidelines provide figures for the recommended nutrient content of an average school meal provided for children over a one-week period. In practical terms this is the total amount of food provided, divided by the number of children eating it, averaged over a week.

	ENERGY	FAT	SAT FATTY ACIDS	CARBO-HYDRATE	NME SUGARS	NSP	PROTEIN	IRON	CALCIUM	VITAMIN A (retinol equivalents)	FOLATE	VITAMIN C
	30% of EAR	Not more than 35% of food energy*	Not more than 11% of food energy*	Not less than 50% of food energy	Not more than 11% of food energy*	Not less than 30% of Calculated Reference Value**	Not less than 30% of RNI	Not less than 40% of RNI	Not less than 35% of RNI	Not less than 30% of RNI	Not less than 40% of RNI	Not less than 35% of RNI
	MJ/kcal	MAX* g	MAX* g	MIN g	MAX* g	MIN g	MIN g	MIN mg	MIN mg	MIN µg	MIN µg	MIN mg
FIRST 5-8 years	2.19MJ 523kcal	20.3	6.4	69.7	15.3	4.2	7.2	3.0	175	150	50	11
MIDDLE 9-13 years	2.46MJ 589kcal	22.9	7.2	78.5	17.3	4.7	10.9	4.9	287	168	72	12
UPPER 14-18 years	2.85MJ 682kcal	26.5	8.3	90.9	18.0	5.5	14.1	5.9	350	189	80	13

SODIUM should be reduced in catering practice.

* As there is no absolute requirement for sugars or fats (except essential fatty acids), these values represent a maximum.

** The Dietary Reference Value for non-starch polysaccharides is 18g for adults, and children should eat proportionately less, based on their lower body size. For pragmatic reasons, this has been calculated for these guidelines as a percentage of the energy recommendation, to give the Calculated Reference Value. The calculated NSP guideline is 8g per 1,000 kcal.

Abbreviations
DRV — Dietary Reference Value
EAR — Estimated Average Requirement
NME SUGARS — Non-milk extrinsic sugars
NSP — Non-starch polysaccharides
RNI — Reference Nutrient Intake
SAT FATTY ACIDS — Saturated fatty acids

Table 19 Nutritional guidelines for school meals FIRST, MIDDLE AND UPPER SCHOOLS: BOYS

These guidelines provide figures for the recommended nutrient content of an average school meal provided for children over a one-week period. In practical terms this is the total amount of food provided, divided by the number of children eating it, averaged over a week.

	ENERGY	FAT	SAT FATTY ACIDS	CARBO-HYDRATE	NME SUGARS	NSP	PROTEIN	IRON	CALCIUM	VITAMIN A (retinol equivalents)	FOLATE	VITAMIN C
	30% of EAR	Not more than 35% of food energy*	Not more than 11% of food energy*	Not less than 50% of food energy	Not more than 11% of food energy*	Not less than 30% of Calculated Reference Value**	Not less than 30% of RNI	Not less than 40% of RNI	Not less than 35% of RNI	Not less than 30% of RNI	Not less than 40% of RNI	Not less than 35% of RNI
	MJ/kcal	MAX* g	MAX* g	MIN g	MAX* g	MIN g	MIN g	MIN mg	MIN mg	MIN µg	MIN µg	MIN mg
FIRST 5-8 years	2.31MJ 553kcal	21.5	6.8	73.7	16.2	4.4	7.2	3.0	175	150	50	11
MIDDLE 9-13 years	2.66MJ 636kcal	24.7	7.8	84.8	18.0	5.1	11.0	4.1	287	168	72	12
UPPER 14-18 years	3.18MJ 762kcal	29.6	9.3	101.6	18.0	6.1	15.0	4.5	350	198	80	13

SODIUM should be reduced in catering practice.

* As there is no absolute requirement for sugars or fats (except essential fatty acids), these values represent a maximum.

** The Dietary Reference Value for non-starch polysaccharides is 18g for adults, and children should eat proportionately less, based on their lower body size. For pragmatic reasons, this has been calculated for these guidelines as a percentage of the energy recommendation, to give the Calculated Reference Value. The calculated NSP guideline is 8g per 1,000 kcal.

Abbreviations
DRV Dietary Reference Value
EAR Estimated Average Requirement
NME SUGARS Non-milk extrinsic sugars
NSP Non-starch polysaccharides
RNI Reference Nutrient Intake
SAT FATTY ACIDS Saturated fatty acids

| Table 20 | Nutritional guidelines for school meals
FIRST, MIDDLE AND UPPER SCHOOLS: GIRLS |

These guidelines provide figures for the recommended nutrient content of an average school meal provided for children over a one-week period. In practical terms this is the total amount of food provided, divided by the number of children eating it, averaged over a week.

	ENERGY	FAT	SAT FATTY ACIDS	CARBO-HYDRATE	NME SUGARS	NSP	PROTEIN	IRON	CALCIUM	VITAMIN A (retinol equivalents)	FOLATE	VITAMIN C
	30% of EAR	Not more than 35% of food energy*	Not more than 11% of food energy*	Not less than 50% of food energy	Not more than 11% of food energy*	Not less than 30% of Calculated Reference Value**	Not less than 30% of RNI	Not less than 40% of RNI	Not less than 35% of RNI	Not less than 30% of RNI	Not less than 40% of RNI	Not less than 35% of RNI
	MJ/kcal	MAX* g	MAX* g	MIN g	MAX* g	MIN g	MIN g	MIN mg	MIN mg	MIN µg	MIN µg	MIN mg
FIRST 5-8 years	2.06MJ 493kcal	19.2	6.0	65.7	14.5	4.0	7.2	3.0	175	150	50	11
MIDDLE 9-13 years	2.26MJ 541kcal	21.0	6.6	72.1	15.9	4.3	10.8	4.9	245	168	72	12
UPPER 14-18 years	2.51MJ 601kcal	23.4	7.3	80.1	17.6	4.8	13.0	5.9	280	180	80	13

SODIUM should be reduced in catering practice.

*   As there is no absolute requirement for sugars or fats (except essential fatty acids), these values represent a maximum.

** The Dietary Reference Value for non-starch polysaccharides is 18g for adults, and children should eat proportionately less, based on their lower body size. For pragmatic reasons, this has been calculated for these guidelines as a percentage of the energy recommendation, to give the Calculated Reference Value. The calculated NSP guideline is 8g per 1,000 kcal.

Abbreviations
DRV   Dietary Reference Value
EAR   Estimated Average Requirement
NME SUGARS   Non-milk extrinsic sugars
NSP   Non-starch polysaccharides
RNI   Reference Nutrient Intake
SAT FATTY ACIDS   Saturated fatty acids

Glossary

BDA	British Dietetic Association
Cafeteria-style service	Cafeteria which provides a choice of dishes from which the children make up a set-price meal
Cash cafeteria	Canteen offering a variety of hot and cold dishes and snacks. Children make their choice and pay for each item.
CCT	Compulsory competitive tendering
CHD	Coronary heart disease
CNG	Community Nutrition Group (of the British Dietetic Association)
COMA	Committee on Medical Aspects of Food Policy
CRV	Calculated Reference Value. Value for non-starch polysaccharides, calculated for these guidelines as a proportion of the adult value, based on a percentage of the adult energy recommendation.
DES	Department of Education and Science. Now replaced by the Department for Education.
DFE	Department for Education. Replaced the Department of Education and Science in 1992.
DHSS	Department of Health and Social Security. Now replaced by the Department of Health and the Department of Social Security
DH	Department of Health. The Department of Health and the Department of Social Security replaced the Department of Health and Social Security in 1989.
DRV	Dietary Reference Value. Replaced Recommended Daily Amounts (RDAs) in 1991. The COMA report replaces RDAs with three figures for requirements for most nutrients: RNI, EAR and LRNI.
DSO	Direct service organisation. In-house school meals catering organisation, usually under the direction of the local authority.
EAR	Estimated Average Requirement. The amount of a nutrient which satisfies 50% of people in a group.
EFA	Essential fatty acid. One which cannot be made in the body and must be supplied by food.

Extrinsic sugar	Any sugar which is not contained within the cell walls of the food. See also NME sugars.
Fibre	See NSP.
Intrinsic sugar	Any sugar which is contained within the cell wall of the food
LEA	Local education authority
LMS	Local management of schools. Introduced under the 1988 Education Reform Act.
LRNI	Lower Reference Nutrient Intake. The amount of the nutrient which is sufficient for the 5% of people in a population who have the lowest needs. Anyone regularly eating less than the LRNI may be at risk of deficiency.
NACNE	National Advisory Committee on Nutrition Education
NME sugars	Non-milk extrinsic sugars. A group of sugars which are neither found naturally incorporated into the cellular structure of food, such as in fresh fruit and vegetables, nor found in milk and milk products. NME sugars include table sugar, sugar added to recipes, and honey, and are found in foods such as confectionery, cakes, biscuits, soft drinks and fruit juices.
NSP	Non-starch polysaccharides ('fibre' as measured by the Englyst method) includes cellulose, insoluble non-cellulosic polysaccharides, and soluble non-cellulosic polysaccharides. Excludes resistant starch and lignin which were previously included in 'fibre' as measured by the Southgate method.
NTD	Neural tube defects (spina bifida and anencephaly)
P/S ratio	Ratio of polyunsaturated fats to saturated fats
RDI	Recommended Daily Intakes of nutrients for the UK (1969). Replaced in 1979 by RDAs.
RDA	Recommended Daily Amount. Recommended nutrient intakes so that the requirements of almost all healthy individuals in a population are met. Replaced in 1991 by DRVs.
RNI	Reference Nutrient Intake. The amount of a nutrient which is sufficient to meet the dietary requirements for 97% of the people in a group. Intakes above this amount will almost certainly be adequate. This corresponds to the previous COMA Recommended Daily Amount (RDA).
SHHD	Scottish Home and Health Department
WHO	World Health Organization